Access Your Online Resources

101 Games for Better Behaviour contains a number of printable online materials, designed to ensure this resource best supports your professional needs.

Go to https://resourcecentre.routledge.com/speechmark and click on the cover of this book.

Answer the question prompt using your copy of the book to gain access to the online content.

'Jenny Mosley is quite simply a legend, whose work has inspired countless teachers and support staff to create the kinds of classrooms and playgrounds in which children can truly thrive. Her bestselling series of *Games* books, written with the equally brilliant Helen Sonnet, has only become more relevant in recent years, as schools across the UK grapple with the many challenges facing children today.'

Jean Gross CBE, *bestselling author and former government Communication Champion for children*

'There is something for everyone, no matter how experienced, to have a go at if they are struggling with particular aspects of behaviour. This book is an excellent "pick up and use" tool for class teachers, pastoral support workers, youth engagement workers and anyone else working with children.'

Helen Sutcliffe, *Headteacher, Brockholes C of E Junior and Infant School*

101 Games for Better Behaviour

This book is full of engaging games and activities that will help children to develop the skills and attributes needed for positive behaviours and effective learning.

Part of the popular *101* series, this practical resource includes a wide range of games that will help children to explore the five key areas: self-awareness, managing feelings, motivation, empathy and social skills. Designed with busy teachers in mind, all activities are adaptable, easy to implement and require little to no additional materials, with resources available to download.

101 Games for Better Behaviour helps children to learn that an effective community is built on co-operation, tolerance and enjoyment. This revised edition features a new introduction mapping games onto the current curriculum, making it the perfect resource for any primary classroom or early years setting.

Jenny Mosley is the founder of Jenny Mosley Training Consultancies and originator of the highly acclaimed 'Quality Circle Time Model' that is used in thousands of early years settings, primary and secondary schools, nationally and internationally. Her unique approach has featured on BBC Television's Teaching Today, Channel 4 and Open University programmes, in addition to the national press and numerous education journals.

Helen Sonnet is a teacher and author with over 30 years of experience working with children with special needs.

101 Games and Activities
Jenny Mosley and Helen Sonnet

101 Games for Better Behaviour
Supporting Feelings and Building Emotional Understanding
ISBN: 9781041083894 (pbk)

101 Games for Self-Esteem
Building Confidence and Motivation
ISBN: 9781041083863 (pbk)

101 Games for Social Skills
Exploring Positive Relationships and Healthy Interactions
ISBN: 9781041084044 (pbk)

101 Activities to Help Children Get On Together
Building Co-operation and Belonging
ISBN: 9781041084068 (pbk)

101 Games for Better Behaviour

Supporting Feelings and Building Emotional Understanding

Revised Edition

Jenny Mosley and Helen Sonnet

LONDON AND NEW YORK

Designed cover image: Getty Images

Revised edition published 2026
by Routledge
4 Park Square, Milton Park, Abingdon, Oxon, OX14 4RN

and by Routledge
605 Third Avenue, New York, NY 10158

Routledge is an imprint of the Taylor & Francis Group, an informa business

© 2026 Jenny Mosley and Helen Sonnet

The right of Jenny Mosley and Helen Sonnet to be identified as authors of this work has been asserted in accordance with sections 77 and 78 of the Copyright, Designs and Patents Act 1988.

Illustrations © Mark Cripps

All rights reserved. The purchase of this copyright material confers the right on the purchasing institution to photocopy or download pages which bear the support material icon and a copyright line at the bottom of the page. No other parts of this book may be reprinted or reproduced or utilised in any form or by any electronic, mechanical, or other means, now known or hereafter invented, including photocopying and recording, or in any information storage or retrieval system, without permission in writing from the publishers.

Trademark notice: Product or corporate names may be trademarks or registered trademarks, and are used only for identification and explanation without intent to infringe.

First edition originally published by LDA 2003

British Library Cataloguing-in-Publication Data
A catalogue record for this book is available from the British Library

ISBN: 978-1-041-08395-5 (hbk)
ISBN: 978-1-041-08389-4 (pbk)
ISBN: 978-1-003-64517-7 (ebk)

DOI: 10.4324/ 9781003645177

Typeset in Interstate
by Deanta Global Publishing Services, Chennai, India

Access the online resources: https://resourcecentre.routledge.com/speechmark

Contents

Acknowledgements	xii
Foreword	xiii
Introduction	xiv

1 Welcome to Our Group — 1

- Great greetings — 2
- The magic beanbag — 3
- Start with a song — 4
- Knowing you, knowing me — 5
- Good to greet — 6
- Mingle — 7
- Shaking circles — 8
- A bouncy 'Hello' — 9
- Further activities — 10

2 Encouraging Emotional Literacy — 11

- The face fits — 12
- How would you feel? — 13
- Drawing on feelings — 14
- Body talk — 15
- Emotional animals — 16
- It's not really funny — 17
- Thinking about feelings — 18
- What could you do? — 20
- Happy or sad? — 21
- Emote-ivate — 22
- Emotional bonding — 23
- Further activities — 24

3 Similarities and Differences — 25

This is me	26
That's handy!	27
Three groups	28
Group talk	29
Thinking of you	30
Body parts	31
Seeking similarities	32
Going undercover	33
One of us	34
Great gifts	35
Further activities	37

4 Personal Strength — 38

Back from the brink	39
There's a storm brewing	40
Volcanoes	41
That drives me so wild!	42
Anger rating	43
I need some space!	44
Sleeping giant	45
Body and mind	46
So strong	47
Step this way	48
Walk tall	50
Further activities	51

5 Strength in Numbers — 53

Step in time	54
Synchronised sequences	55
Tuned in	56
What would you do?	57
The call of the wild	58

	Agreeing as a group	59
	A roll of the dice	60
	On cue	61
	Legs eleven	62
	Riddle-me-ree	63
	Further activities	64
6	**Learning to Listen**	**65**
	Follow me	66
	Behind your back	67
	This way or that way?	68
	That's my cue	69
	Silent but deadly	70
	Let's get quizzical	71
	Left, right	72
	The ski run	73
	Get to the point	74
	Think on your feet	75
	Further activities	76
7	**Nurturing Imaginative Thought**	**77**
	An alien came	78
	Predictions	79
	Come out, timid alien	80
	The lucky star	81
	Rewards of our dreams	82
	I've got your number	83
	Counting on you	84
	School playtime	85
	Don't destroy our school!	86
	Up the ladder	87
	Good to great	88
	Further activities	89

8 Energetic Games for Excess Energy — 90

- Breaching the wall — 91
- Chase the chair — 92
- Keep your head — 93
- Bean and gone — 94
- Two's company — 95
- Mixed messages — 96
- A soft-ball sandwich — 97
- The mouse, the tree and the wind — 98
- At the races — 99
- Take your partner — 100
- Further activities — 101

9 Games to Promote Calm — 102

- Best foot forward — 103
- Fast and slow — 104
- Fighting the marshmallow — 105
- The spring has sprung — 106
- Walk the talk — 107
- Don't panic! — 108
- A sprinting six — 109
- Running water — 110
- The golden dome — 111
- Floating — 112
- Further activities — 113

10 Games to Promote Positive Group Dynamics — 114

- The en-chanting class — 115
- A good word — 116
- Triangular poems — 117
- The animal questival — 118
- Top ten — 119

What did I do?	*120*
The enchanted forest	*121*
Colour coded	*122*
Down in the woods	*123*
It's a celebration	*124*
Further activities	*125*
Printable Materials	**127**
The face fits	*128*
How would you feel?	*129*
It's not really funny	*130*
Thinking about feelings	*131*
What could you do?	*132*
Emote-ivate	*133*
This is me	*134*
Three groups	*135*
Seeking similarities	*136*
Anger rating	*137*
What would you do?	*138*
Left, right	*139*
The mouse, the tree and the wind	*140*
Training and Resources	**141**

Acknowledgements

We would like to thank all the schools that so willingly try out games both in the classrooms and the playgrounds. Holbrook Primary School is very near us and they are always up for volunteering their children to try out new ideas.

We are very thankful to Taylor & Francis for their enthusiasm in ensuring all our books reach many new younger teachers. Jane Madeley is a very positive, patient and thoughtful editor.

Last, we would like to thank our grandchildren for enjoying lots of the games with us, although we both admit it is easier sometimes to help other people's children than to help our own family, he he!!

Jenny Mosley and Helen Sonnet

Foreword

Jenny Mosley is quite simply a legend, whose work has inspired countless teachers and support staff to create the kinds of classrooms and playgrounds in which children can truly thrive. Her bestselling series of *Games* books, written with the equally brilliant Helen Sonnet, has only become more relevant in recent years, as schools across the UK grapple with the many challenges facing children today.

Games promote a sense of belonging in a class or group. And belonging (or lack of it) is emerging as a key issue affecting children's learning, behaviour and attendance. When we experience feelings of belonging to a group, our body produces a hormone soup that makes us feel calm and able to focus. Conversely, if we are unsure whether we belong, we are anxious, constantly monitoring the environment for cues as to whether or how we can fit in. Creating a cohesive class, where there is a sense of group identity, avoids this and frees children to concentrate on learning.

The games in this book also build essential social and emotional skills, like self-awareness, self-regulation, empathy and the social skills of co-operation and conflict resolution. Research shows us that teaching these skills can make a significant contribution to attainment, as well as to a range of other important outcomes, from mental health to employability.

Flexible in their use – from playground to start and end of day, PE warm-ups or circle time – the game ideas that Jenny and Helen share here should play a part in every child's day. Some people might argue that this is a waste of learning time. The evidence, however, suggests otherwise. I cannot recommend these books strongly enough.

Jean Gross CBE
Bestselling author and former government
Communication Champion for children

Introduction

This book is packed with games designed for anyone and everyone who loves to have fun – whether you're leading a group, building a team or just bringing people together.

Emerging research keeps highlighting the importance of play, fun and games. 'Studies have shown that playing positively impacts the brain, triggering the release of endorphins, reducing cortisol levels and fostering relaxation. Playful adults are more likely to employ positive coping mechanisms such as acceptance and reframing in stressful situations' (Stuart Brown, founder of National Institute of Play, 2025).

If you're a group leader who believes in the power of play, you will find ways to adapt, remix and expand on what's inside. Let the fun begin!

In its Guidance Report (2021) for Improving Social and Emotional Learning in Primary Schools, the Education Endowment Foundation (EEF) describes the core behaviour competency as self-management; the ability to successfully regulate one's emotions, thoughts and behaviours in different situations – to manage stress, control impulses and motivate oneself. The ability to set and work towards personal and academic goals. Control your impulses, self-discipline and self-motivation.

We have all been in situations in which we have felt restless, anxious or downright angry, and have been aware that these difficult feelings have arisen mainly as a response to something outside ourselves. Mature adults have learned that it is crucial to take control of such unsettling emotions, and have enough life experience to be able to identify the source of their disquiet and, hopefully, to take appropriate measures such as distancing themselves from it. These are skills that many children still need to learn. Their experience of emotions is different from our own, in the sense that they are much more likely to react instinctively, and may be taken by surprise when emotions overwhelm them.

This book is designed to show you how behavioural skills can be taught in an enjoyable way by engaging children's attention in engrossing, interactive games and activities. Some of the games help children to recognise and manage emotions in themselves and others, while promoting effective listening and thinking skills, and recognising that we are all different. Other games help children to understand the difference between outer and inner strength and learn how they can become more independent and self-determining in their actions and reactions. There are also sections of games that help to destress a group or to provide a positive outlet for excess energy, both helpful skills when it comes to managing our behaviour.

Children come to you to be challenged and stretched – two words that imply a certain amount of pressure and stress. They need to learn how to co-operate as part of a group, and how to work with enthusiasm to the best of their ability. In other words, it is our job to motivate and encourage young children to make positive changes.

Another part of our job is to make sure that they all feel safe and confident at the same time. The art of excellent teaching is to create a balance between the two. This can only be achieved when you, as leader, create a sense of community in which hard work takes place in a positive, caring atmosphere, where every child feels valued and the possibility of distress is minimised. You need to be watchful and calm the children before tension or anxiety slips into discord or vulnerability.

This book shows you how to build a strong community where learning begins with a warm welcome, and in which moments of pleasure are planned into each day to relax and revitalise you and your children. The games in this book encourage children to appreciate that working together in a cooperative manner can increase the effectiveness of their efforts and enhance their achievements. Other games help to build good group dynamics through activities that encourage children to become better acquainted with one another while having fun. This knowledge helps them to develop loyalties and creates effective group cohesion and strength, building tolerance that balances any discord which could result in behavioural tension.

The pace of the games is varied – some are fast and exciting, while others are calm and reflective. You can choose the game that suits your particular needs and current requirements. All of the games have been successfully tried and tested. It is a good idea to note down those that your children particularly enjoy so that you can quickly refer to them.

You can either work through the book exploring the themed sections in detail with your group, or find games that suit a specific purpose. Whichever option you choose, have fun. Enjoy each other's company and the benefits of a happier, better-behaved and more emotionally aware group.

1 Welcome to Our Group

One valuable way to encourage better behaviour is to ensure that you bring a group together purposefully and nurture a sense of belonging at the beginning of a session. This could be the start of a day, morning or afternoon; or before a particular lesson, Circle Time or group task.

Joining in an activity that makes everyone feel welcomed helps children to be positive about themselves and less anxious about the challenges ahead.

A short welcome ritual doesn't take much time, and pays dividends as it helps everyone to feel part of a bonded group that has come together to learn. For some children, the welcome will have an even greater importance because it offers them a space to stop, think and leave any troubles behind them at the door by focusing fully on all the interesting activities that you have ready for them that day.

All the games in this section concentrate on greetings that promote the pleasure of coming together in a place where everyone works as part of a team and no one is left out.

Great greetings

A simple beginning game to welcome every child.

Resources

A list of greetings devised with the children, on a flipchart. This can be generated before the game, and reused and added to.

What to do

Everyone stands in a circle, each with a chair or cushion behind them. Display the list of greetings to refer to. They could include:

- a high five
- a handshake
- a salaam (low bow, palm of right hand on forehead)
- a bow
- touched palms
- gentle handclapping
- a raised right hand, palm forward
- hands together as in prayer, with a small bow

Choose a child to begin the game by crossing the circle to greet another child. If the greeting involves a response, the second child gives this in return. The child giving the greeting then says 'Hello' to the second child by name. The greeted child replies in the same way. The first child returns to their place and sits down. The second child moves across to greet a third child. The game continues until all the children but one are seated. The last child standing finishes the game by saying, 'Hello, everyone.'

Comments

This works best if children use recognised forms of greeting rather than ones they have made up themselves. Bear in mind that some children may have difficulty from a personal or cultural perspective with greetings that involve touch. If you do not have chairs available, the children can sit on the floor after their turn.

The magic beanbag

This game will dispel any sleepiness because every child needs to be alert and on their toes. It involves every member of the group and never fails to gain everyone's attention.

Resources

A small beanbag or see 'Comments' below where we suggest rolling a large ball.

What to do

Ask everyone to stand in a circle. Choose one child to stand in the centre of the circle with the beanbag. This child throws the beanbag to a child in the circle, greeting that child, and adding the child's name. The second child catches the beanbag and then throws it back to the child in the centre, greeting them in the same way. Each child should receive the beanbag from the child in the centre once during the game. The child in the centre can vary the greeting from child to child, with the recipient responding in the same manner. They could use 'Hello', 'Hi!', 'Good morning' or 'Good afternoon'. You could explore and use greetings in other languages, either represented in your group or not.

Comments

Each child could sit down once they have returned the beanbag to the child in the centre after their greeting, and the child in the middle could be asked to greet someone who is standing each time. You could repeat this activity at the end of a session, when the children could say 'Goodbye' to one another.

Emphasise that the beanbag should be thrown sensibly and gently to each recipient. You could also say that it doesn't matter if a child drops the beanbag. If you think that throwing a beanbag may be difficult for your group, ask the children to roll a large ball to one another instead.

Start with a song

This welcoming game requires concentration and focused attention, and will help to prepare your children for the day's lessons.

Resources

None.

What to do

Call the children together to form a circle. Using the tune of 'One Man Went to Mow', sing a song that includes everyone's name and a final greeting. The words of the song could be as follows:

John went to school, went to school this morning,
John and Jessima went to school, went to school this morning.

Choose the name of a child in your group to begin the song. When you come to the second line, add the name of the child on the first child's left. Continue round the circle, adding the next child's name to the second line of the song. Add a chant of 'Hello, everybody' when you complete the final line of the song.

Comments

Try different well-known tunes and have fun trying to fit the names in. You could try 'Happy Birthday to … (name of a child)'. Some children never get invited to parties. You can create a pretend party where one child a week has invitations to give out to all the other children, has 'Happy Birthday' sung to them, chooses their favourite games and maybe a gift could be given from all the children. Some songs can be quite tricky when it comes to fitting the words to the tune. Practise them yourself beforehand.

Knowing you, knowing me

This greeting game places an emphasis on what people have in common and is a good bonding activity.

Resources

None.

What to do

Ask everyone to make a circle. Call out a category, for example:

- Everyone who has a brother.
- Everyone with black hair.
- Everyone who likes dogs.
- Everyone who enjoys reading poetry.

Each child who identifies themselves with the named category goes into the centre of the circle and verbally greets up to three other children who are also in the circle. They could use 'Hello', 'Hi!', 'Good morning' or 'Good afternoon', along with the child's name. They then return to their place in the circle and a different category is called.

As children become familiar with this game, you could ask some of them to nominate appropriate categories.

Comments

This game is particularly useful if you play it prior to an activity exploring the similarities and differences between group members. By carefully choosing your categories, you can highlight discussion points for this activity. Devising a name for your group with its members, such as 'The Friendly Force', can highlight similarities and differences and the need for tolerance.

Good to greet

This simple chant is a very effective opening ritual for the beginning of the day or any session thereafter.

Resources

None.

What to do

Gather the children in a standing circle. Choose a child in the group to begin the chant. Explain that you will say the first line of the chant as below, using that child's name, and then everyone should clap once. You then sit down. The named child repeats the sentence, substituting the name of another child in the group, again followed by a clap from everyone:

Group leader: A clap for Tia, then pass it on. (clap)
Tia: A clap for Zac, then pass it on. (clap)
Zac: A clap for Bradley, then pass it on. (clap)

Once a child has said their line, they sit down. The final child to be named says the line that follows:

Final child: A clap for everyone. (clap)

Comments

The aim of this game is to keep the action flowing. Encourage the children to name the next child quickly so that the chant isn't interrupted.

A variation of this game is for the children to clap the syllables of the chosen child's name after the line is said.

Mingle

This is a good game for new groups or to create a positive start to a session with an established group.

Resources

Tambourine.

What to do

The children move about in the centre of the room. When you bang the tambourine, they stop and greet the person nearest to them. If they are in an established group, they can greet one another by name. If they do not know the other members of the group, they should introduce themselves to the person nearest to them as part of their greeting. They could use the following sentence as a template:

Hello, my name is . . .

When they have completed their greeting, they mingle again. Continue in this way for several more encounters.

Comments

Encourage the children to greet a different person each time. To make the encounters more interesting, the children can tell each other their favourite meal after they have said hello. You could change the theme for each encounter to cover other favourite things and to keep interest high. Another variation is to play lively music while the children are moving about; the children stop and greet someone when you stop the music.

Shaking circles

This novel game gives energetic purpose to the greeting process.

Resources

None.

What to do

Divide the children into two equal groups. One forms a circle facing outwards; the other a circle round the first circle, facing inwards. Tell the outer circle to move slowly round in a clockwise direction. As a child in the outer circle passes a child in the inner circle, they shake hands and say hello. Continue until each child in the outer circle has greeted each child in the inner circle.

Comments

If you know that certain children in your group will refuse, on this occasion, to shake hands with each other, make sure that they are in the same group so that they will not come into contact.

You could vary the greeting for a change or to accommodate children who find this form of touch difficult for cultural or religious reasons. Other greetings you could use are as follows:

- a salaam (low bow, palm of right hand on the forehead)
- a bow
- gentle handclapping
- a raised right hand, palm forward
- hands together as in prayer, with a small bow

Once they are familiar with this game, they can tell one fact about themselves to each person they greet. You could suggest a category (e.g. favourite animals) before the game begins. If you make the wording broad, children can give different answers as they progress. At the end, ask for volunteers to repeat a fact they have learnt about another child in the group.

A bouncy 'Hello'

This is an enjoyable way to perform greetings in an established group.

Resources

A large, light bouncy ball, well inflated.

What to do

Divide the children into two equal groups. Arrange the groups in two parallel lines. They need to face each other, a metre or two apart, depending on their ball skills and the space available. A child at the end of one line begins by bouncing the ball carefully to the child standing opposite them in the other line. Before they do this, they say 'Hello', and name the child. The child who receives the ball then bounces it to the child in the opposite line next to the one who bounced the ball to them, after saying the greeting. This zigzag pattern continues down the line to the last child.

Comments

If the children have good ball skills, or as they become more confident, you can add a further element of fun: link a different greeting to various ways of passing the ball. For example:

- 'Hello …' can be linked with bouncing the ball once.
- 'Have a good day' can be linked to a double bounce (the child opposite must wait for the ball to bounce twice).
- 'Good afternoon' can be linked to a chest pass.
- 'Nice to see you' can be linked to an underarm pass.

The children will need to concentrate on the type of greeting used so they know how to prepare to receive the ball. You could introduce some greetings in other languages, either represented in your group or not. Younger children can sit facing each other and roll the ball backwards and forwards.

Further activities

Official greeter

Choose different children for the morning and afternoon sessions to be official greeters as the other children enter the room. They could have a prepared speech, such as, 'I'm the group's official morning/afternoon greeter today and I'd like to welcome you all into class and wish you a good morning/afternoon'.

Pass a handshake

The children stand in a circle and pass a handshake from child to child in a clockwise direction. They then pass a smile in the opposite direction.

Insect greetings

This is an enjoyable greeting for younger children. Each child holds one of their index fingers either side of their head to represent antennae. They walk around, greeting other insects by wiggling their antennae at them and saying hello.

Racing greeting

Divide the children into two teams. Each team stands in a line facing forwards. The front child of each team should be level with a mark on the floor. The children behind each team leader space themselves out so that there are equal gaps between them. On the command 'Go', the lead child in each team turns and weaves their way in and out of the line of children behind them, through the spaces created earlier. As they pass each member of their team, they shake their hand. When they reach the end of their line, they join it, leaving a space in front of them. The line moves forwards to the mark. The child now at the front of the line repeats the process. This continues until each child in the team has had a turn. The first team to complete their greeting is the winner.

2 Encouraging Emotional Literacy

Developing the ability to recognise emotions in themselves and others is a key factor in promoting better behaviour. Emotions set the tone of all of our experiences, and are very closely connected to our level of motivation and our beliefs about our ability to learn and succeed.

Some children are not very skilled at reading the emotions of others correctly. They seem unable to link certain facial expressions and body postures to the relevant emotions. This can lead to difficulties and confrontations. This section of games focuses on their own facial expressions and those of others, and explores appropriate emotions for given situations.

The face fits

This game focuses on facial expressions.

Resources

A flipchart, a marker pen, some Blu Tack® and a photocopy (or printout) of the facial expressions on page 128, enlarged if possible. Cut the photocopy up into the individual boxes, each with a face in it. The emotions depicted are as follows: happy, sad, excited, angry, surprised, worried, frightened and jealous.

What to do

Write the names of the emotions above on the flipchart. Ask the children to sit in a circle, and show them those words. Next, show them the faces, one at a time, and then lay the photocopies on the floor in the centre, face up. Point to an emotion on the list and ask which face shows that emotion. After discussion about the most appropriate face and why, ask a volunteer to stick it next to the appropriate word on the flipchart. To explore how the whole body reacts to a particular emotion, ask the volunteer to move in a way that depicts the emotion being explored as they pick up the face.

Ask for volunteers to choose secretly an expression from the flipchart to act out. They then show this expression to the rest of the group, who have to try to guess which emotion is being shown. This could also be done in pairs in the circle.

Comments

As a follow-up, ask the children to study the faces on the flipchart carefully. Choose an emotion from the list. Ask them to make a face depicting it, looking at each other. Repeat this with other emotions on the flipchart. Ask what features help them to recognise the emotion. When they have established that the eyes and mouth give the clearest clues, ask them to describe how these features form the emotions.

How would you feel?

This game encourages children to consider carefully the emotions that often accompany given situations.

Resources

A photocopy (or printout) of the list of situations on page 129 and photocopies of the facial expressions on page 128, enough for one each for the number of groups you decide upon. If you have the time to laminate the photocopies of facial expressions before cutting them into sets, they can be used time and time again.

What to do

Put the children into groups of two to four, depending on the size of your initial group. Give each group a set of facial expressions. Read a statement from the photocopy of page 129 and ask the groups to discuss which facial expression in their set they feel most accurately reflects how someone might feel in that situation. Once they have agreed, ask each group to hold up the facial expression they have picked and to say what emotion it represents, after which you re-read the statement.

Comments

Stress that the emotion to be nominated is the one that each group feels is most likely to be associated with the situation in question. You may find that different groups hold up different emotions.

Some groups may find it difficult to agree amongst themselves, so explain that a vote may be necessary if agreement cannot be reached. If groups choose different cards for a given situation, discuss how different people react in different ways, but that it is good to have a general idea of how people are likely to react. Explain that sometimes you can experience a range of emotions and one might give rise to another – for example, embarrassment could lead to anger.

Drawing on feelings

This game helps the children to recognise emotions.

Resources

A flipchart, a marker pen, paper, pencils and coloured pencils or felt pens.

What to do

Discuss emotions that are the opposite of each other; for example:

- happy/sad
- frightened/courageous
- angry/calm
- lonely/popular
- nervous/confident

Record these pairs on the flipchart. Arrange the children into groups of up to four, depending on the size of your original group. Give out paper and pencils/pens for each child. Ask each child to choose an emotion from the flipchart and then to show this in the form of a pattern, shape or colour (or any combination of these). It does not matter if members of the same group choose the same emotion. Ask the children to think carefully about feelings they associate with their chosen emotion and to let this determine the shape and colour of their picture. When they have done this, go round the groups and ask them to hold up their compositions, each saying which emotion their picture depicts. Try to include time to compare the artwork done in the groups, and for each child to say how they produced their picture.

Comments

Encourage the children to use descriptive words to explain how they composed their work. For example, anger could be hard, spiky and red, while lonely could be grey, small and cracked. You may want to include rounds in which you give groups a specific emotion to explore to avoid some emotions being overlooked.

Body talk

This game helps children to learn about how to read another person's emotional state by the way they move and act.

Resources

None.

What to do

Ask the children to imagine that they are feeling really happy, then each think of a short mime to signify something that makes them happy (e.g. unwrapping a present, eating a favourite meal). Ask each child to perform their mime to the rest. Get volunteers to suggest what each mime might be about. Next, put the children into pairs and ask them to prepare a mime of something that makes them happy. Get pairs to perform their mimes and ask the others to guess what is going on. Finally, put the children into larger groups of up to six, depending on the size of your original group. Ask each group to form a tableau depicting a group activity that makes them happy (e.g. a parachute game, a birthday party). After practice, ask each group to perform their tableau and for suggestions from the rest about what is being performed. In all cases, discuss how the children's expressions and body language give a clear indication of their emotional state.

Comments

If you think the children will find it difficult to agree what to perform in pairs or groups, brainstorm ideas and write them on a flipchart beforehand, then ask them to choose from this list.

This game can be used to explore more difficult emotions such as anger, sadness and fear. These will need careful handling and should perhaps be limited to school events, accompanied by discussion about how to improve these situations.

Emotional animals

This game helps children to see that emotions can be expressed in many different metaphorical ways.

Resources

A flipchart and a marker pen. A list of emotions written on a flipchart, such as *angry*, *sad*, *lonely*, *happy*, *excited*, *frightened* and *proud*. A selection of animal pictures. (This is not essential but is a handy reference point. You could cut the pictures out of old wildlife magazines, print them from the internet or display some books from the school/local library.)

What to do

Write a selection of emotions suggested by the group on the flipchart. Choose one as an example and select an animal (from your selection, if you have made one) that you consider fits that emotion; for example, as *brave* as a lion. If you are using a preselected list of animals, you may have to help the children to think of one if those on the list do not fit the emotion. Ask the children to volunteer any other animals they think fit that emotion. You could record these on the flipchart. Ask a child who volunteers an animal to explain why they have made that choice. Repeat this for the other emotions on the list, asking a child to choose the first animal for each emotion. Younger children might like to act out the animal for the others to guess.

Comments

You could repeat this game with other categories such as food, weather and colours.

It's not really funny

This game draws the children's attention to the emotional outcome of certain behaviours.

Resources

An enlarged photocopy (or printout) of page 130.

What to do

Ask the children to describe what is happening in the photocopied scene. Encourage them to explain how each child shown might be feeling. Some groups may go beyond the surface emotion and discuss the deeper emotions of the child doing the tripping or the tensions of the onlookers. The discussions should be influenced by your school's anti-bullying policy.

Ask the children about times when they were unintentionally unkind. How did they realise that someone had been upset? This discussion should bring out the need to consider your actions beforehand by your imagining how you would feel in another's situation. The activity could be done using 'hot-seating'. Choose a scene mentioned in the discussion. Ask for volunteers to take the roles and sit on the 'hot seat'. In turn, they are asked by the others about their actions and feelings. You may like to establish rules about fair treatment of the person in the hot seat and explain that they need to be true to the character they represent. If you choose this option, de-role the children at the end by finishing the game on a positive note. Get everyone into a circle and pass a handshake and then a smile round.

Comments

A suggested script to help de-role children: 'Close your eyes, breathe calmly through your nose to the count of three and out of your mouth to the count of three. Let's gently go back to reality … we are not the people we have been playing. We are a great group of people who are trying to find ways to be thoughtful. Each one of us is unique. Some of you are funny or you're a good listener, kind and quick thinking. Each one of you is special … we are the Fun Friendly Force'.

Thinking about feelings

This game encourages children to realise that the quality of our interpersonal relationships impacts on our sense of well-being.

Resources

An enlarged photocopy (or printout) of page 131.

What to do

Ask them to describe the photocopied scene, and say how they think each child is feeling. The comments may introduce the label of 'bully', and you may want to clarify your school's definition of bullying. Following the Anti-Bullying Alliance guidance, you could give the following as a useful definition

> Bullying is when someone keeps hurting another person on purpose, and the person being hurt has a hard time stopping it. It can be hitting, mean words, or trying to make someone feel bad. Bullying can happen in person or on the internet, and usually, the bully has more power, like being stronger or having more friends.
>
> (Anti-Bullying Alliance, 2025)

Initial comments about the bully in the scene may focus on the fact that they feel glad about the outcome of their actions. You may need to help them to think about other possibilities, such as that the bully reacts in this way because they are lonely, frustrated or being bullied themselves. You could use hot-seating, with some children volunteering to take on the roles in the scene and answer questions put by the rest. You may like to establish rules about fair treatment of the person in the hot seat and explain that they need to be true to the character they represent. A few additional children can stand behind the volunteer to help with answers. De-role the children with a positive game such as fruit bowl. If you choose four fruits, for example apple, banana, pear, grape, and then assign each child a fruit by going around the circle and repeating the fruits in order. There should be an almost even number of children assigned to each fruit. Then you call out one of the fruits and these children change place. You can also call out 'fruit bowl' and they all change places. By only doing four fruits it shouldn't get too chaotic.

When they're finished and sitting peacefully – de-role. We are not the people in the picture, we are just a great group who like thinking and understanding. We also love playing games because we are the Fun Friendly Force.

Comments

Encourage the children to realise that bullying is harmful to the bully, robbing them of emotions such as empathy and compassion.

What could you do?

This is a game to be played in pairs. The children in each pair work together to consider responsible and empathic ways of responding to situations.

Resources

Photocopies (or printouts) of page 132, one for each pair.

What to do

Put the children into pairs and give each pair a photocopy of page 132, showing four scenes. Tell the children they will have ten minutes to look at the scenes and think of helpful things that they could say or do to improve each situation. Tell them to be realistic in their suggestions, and that they must not include any responses that will escalate the problem. After ten minutes, call the children into a circle and talk about each situation. Gather suggestions from a range of pairs. You might like to pause at times to discuss the possible outcomes of suggestions made. You could agree on an action plan for putting a scene right before moving on to the next one.

You could join pairs together to make groups of four to six, depending on the size of your group. Give each group a scene that you have been discussing and ask them to practise a role play of the agreed action plan to show its successful application. After ten minutes, gather the groups together into a circle again and ask different groups to perform their role play.

Comments

It would be wise to consider the initial pairings carefully to ensure that those children who might suggest inappropriate responses are with children who will have a positive influence on them.

Happy or sad?

This game fosters a feeling of collaboration among pairs of children as they discuss their responses to situations.

Resources

Each pair will need a small ball of string or wool.

What to do

Put the children into mixed-ability pairs and give them a ball of string or wool. Ask the children to think of situations in which they have felt sad – for example, when a toy was broken, they fell out with a friend or they did something wrong. The children take it in turns in their pairs to name a sad situation. The first child in each pair to do so holds the ball of string/wool. As they name a situation, they pass it to their partner while holding onto the end. Their partner responds with a situation they have chosen. They pass the ball to their partner while holding onto the loop created. The string/wool unravels, creating a web.

After sharing several sad situations, change to sharing happy situations. The child holding the ball of string/wool in each pair shares the first happy situation. As they pass the ball to their partner, they wind the strand of string/wool back round the ball. This process of sharing happy situations continues until the ball is wound up again. When all the balls are wound up, bring the pairs back together and ask each child to share a happy situation that their partner told them about.

Comments

Talk to the children about words that describe happy/sad situations. Words that describe happy situations could include *pleasant, exciting, loving, caring, friendly* and so on. Words that describe sad situations could include *gloomy, grim, unhappy, upsetting* and so on.

Emote-ivate

This is a game for children to play with a partner to explore different facial expressions.

Resources

A photocopy (or printout) of page 133 and a pencil for each pair.

What to do

Put the children into mixed-ability pairs. Give each pair a photocopy of page 133 and a pencil. Tell them that they have ten minutes to look at the photocopied sheet and to match the emotions written on the sheet to the children in the picture. Encourage the children to share their views constructively with their partner and to reach agreement on their choices. After ten minutes, call the children into a circle and lead a discussion in which the pairs share their results. This could be done with one pair of children sharing a finding and then asking who else agreed by asking for a show of hands. If some pairs had made a different choice, this could lead to interesting discussion about what they chose and why.

Comments

Ask the children which expressions they found hardest to read and why they think this was.

Emotional bonding

This is a game for small groups, to help children recognise typical classroom situations that can give rise to both positive and negative feelings.

Resources

A ball of string, paper and pencils.

What to do

Put the children into groups of four or five, depending on the size of the original group, and give each group a piece of paper and a pencil. Appoint a scribe and speaker for each group. Tell the groups they have ten minutes to think of situations in the classroom that make them feel good; for example, being praised for good work or behaviour, finding a lesson interesting, helping somebody who needs support, reading a good book, getting something right in your head and so on. Each scribe is to note their group's suggestions. After ten minutes, call the children into a standing circle to compare the notes. Make sure the children remain in their group.

Each group's speaker should share their findings with the circle.

Mark a line on the floor using the ball of string, label one end of it 'agree' and the other 'disagree'. As each group shares their ideas, the other children stand in a position on the string line that represents how they feel about each situation as it is mentioned. For example, school productions may make some very happy, whereas they might fill others with dread. Ask the children to move into their groups again and repeat what they have done, this time noting down situations that give rise to negative emotions – being told off unfairly, another child being mean to them and so on. Call the groups back after ten minutes and repeat the group activity.

Comments

Ask the children if their discussions affected their moods – did they feel happier when discussing positive situations? Use the discussion to explore how what we think and say influences how we feel.

Further activities

Role play

Explore role plays that involve strong emotions: for example, a child has an argument with a parent about the time they go to bed, or the feelings that might arise if a child were chosen to take part in a talent competition on television. Such scenarios could be explored in groups, with different characters experiencing different emotions. Their actions and responses could be explored in discussion afterwards.

Hand signals

This is an enjoyable activity that children can complete in small groups. Ask them to think of a variety of hand signals that denote certain emotions – for example, *angry*, *sad*, *happy*, *scared* and so on. Tell the children to try to link the nature of a hand signal to how the related emotion makes them feel. Let the groups demonstrate their signals to each other.

Spinners

Make hexagonal spinners out of thin card. Use plastic two-dimensional hexagons as a template. Be careful when you insert a pencil through the centre of the shape. It is best to push the pencil through the card into a ball of modelling clay on the desktop. Ask the children to write the name of a different emotion on each segment of their spinner. When they use their spinner, they must think of a situation that provokes the emotion that the spinner stops on.

Reference

Anti-Bullying Alliance, 2025. *Definition of bullying*. [online] Available at: Anti-Bullying Alliance. https://anti-bullyingalliance.org.uk/tools-information/all-about-bullying/understanding-bullying/definition (Accessed 7 July 2025).

3 Similarities and Differences

When children feel a real sense of belonging to a group, they are less likely to behave in a way that will alienate that group. This section of games acknowledges the uniqueness of individuals, while focusing on the similarities between people and the benefits of including others in a group.

This is me

This game celebrates the uniqueness of each individual, even though some children's responses may be similar.

Resources

Enough photocopies (or printouts) of page 134 and pencils for each child in the group. If you have children with writing difficulties in your group, this game is best played when you have additional adult support.

What to do

Give each child a photocopy of page 134 and allow them a reasonable amount of time to complete the sections on the sheet. When the responses have all been completed, either during this session or a later one, call the children together into a circle and let them compare what they have written. This could be done by using each sentence as a circle round. Start each round with a different person. Use prompts to help them investigate how commonality and differences make each of us unique and valuable.

Comments

Make a wall display of the completed fact sheets, including self-portraits of each child. Alternatively, using a digital camera, you could take photos of the children and display the print-outs with the fact sheets.

That's handy!

This game looks at both the similarities and the differences between people.

Resources

Two or three ink pads, and enough paper, scissors and pencils for one for each group.

What to do

Ask each child to draw around one of their hands and cut out the resultant outline. Using the ink pads, each child makes prints of their fingers and thumb in the relevant places on their paper cutout. They may need to wipe their hands after using the ink. Let the children compare the different patterns of their prints with those of a couple of other children. Ask each child to write their name and three things that they use their hands for on the palm of their cutout; for example, writing, catching balls, holding books, playing games on their console/tablet. Bring the children together into a circle and put all the cut-out hands into the centre. Ask a volunteer to choose one at random. Ask them to read out the comments, excluding the name, and see if the children can guess whose hand it is. Repeat with others.

Comments

Talk to the children about the similarities in their hands – that is, they all use them to perform certain tasks and all hands are made up of bones, skin, muscles, nerves and so on. Explain that every fingerprint is a totally unique signature for that particular person – they are all different and belong to only one person, illustrating how each of us is unique and special.

Three groups

This is an enjoyable game that focuses on the benefits of establishing an inclusive group.

Resources

The story on page 135 (photocopied or downloaded and printed if you wish).

What to do

Ask the children to sit in a circle. Read through the story about the three groups on page 135. Divide the children into the three groups by going round the circle naming child 1 a Booja, child 2 a Lalli, and child 3 a Widgell and so on. Read the story again. Each time a child hears their group name mentioned, they stand up. On the third reading, each time a child hears their group name they stand up and swap places with another member of their group

Comments

Discuss with the children how first impressions can be misleading, and taking time to get to know someone fully can bring all sorts of nice surprises. There may be groups of children within your class that could learn lessons from the end of this story. You could explore this by discussing what the Lallis and Boojas might have missed out on had the Widgells not taken action.

Similarities and Differences 29

Group talk

This game continues the theme of the three groups from page 28 by building on each group's particular identity.

Resources

Paper, pencils and coloured pencils.

What to do

Remind the children of the work done on the three groups from page 28. You could re-read the story on page 135. Ask the children to get into the three groups of Boojas, Lallis and Widgells that they were previously in. Give each group paper and a range of pencils. Appoint a spokesperson, an artist and a scribe for each group. Give the groups ten minutes to decide what their group members look like – costume, hairstyles and so on. After this, the artist in each group can get on with drawing one of their group. In the meantime, the rest of the group decide on the words for *boy*, *girl*, *school*, *dinner* and *dog* in their language.

Ask the groups to describe the food that they would eat at one of their group's celebrations. The scribe records this. After ten minutes, call the groups into a circle to discuss their results. Get each group's spokesperson to share their findings, and each group's artist to share their impression of how one of their group members would look. Look for any similarities between the groups' choices. Ask them what factors influenced their choices.

Comments

If there is disagreement about any of the choices, the groups must make a choice by a democratic vote to avoid an argument. It may be worth establishing this rule before the activity begins, so that a system that everyone subscribes to is in place.

Thinking of you

A good game to emphasise the uniqueness of each child.

Resources

A sheet of paper and a pencil.

What to do

Gather the children into a circle. Ask one child to think of another child in the circle and write their name on a piece of paper so no one else can see it. They could leave the circle briefly to do this. This ensures that the child doesn't forget whom they have picked or later change their mind. The child gives you the piece of paper so you have an idea of how they should answer the subsequent questions.

Ask other children in the circle to think of questions they could ask the child who started, in order to identify the chosen child. These questions could require a 'Yes' or 'No' answer; for example, 'Is this person a girl?', 'Does this person have blonde hair?' or 'Is this person wearing blue socks?' They could also ask more specific questions, such as, 'Does this person have a brother in Beech class?' and 'Is this person in the school football team?' You could agree a set number of questions, after which the other children can guess the chosen child.

Children could put their hands up when they have a question to ask. Either you or the child who picked the chosen child can select children to ask questions. When the correct identity has been found, a different child can choose someone to identify.

Comments

Tell the children not to look directly at the person they are thinking about or they will give the game away. Discuss with the children how, although we all share some things in common, each person is unique in specific details.

Body parts

This game looks at the possibility of sharing ideas effectively with others.

Resources

None.

What to do

Ask the children to sit in a circle and to think of a part of their body they like and why (e.g. their legs because they are good at running, their brains because they are good at thinking). Ask the children to complete the following sentence in their heads.

I like my ... because ...

Choose a child to begin a round using the sentence stem. The children could hold a competition in which individuals volunteer to be different body parts, stating why they are the best. For example:

I am the legs. I am the most important because without me you wouldn't get anywhere. I can take you to good things and away from danger. I help you enjoy many sports. Vote for me.

At the end of the volunteers' speeches, the other children vote to determine the best body part. Do be sensitive to the needs of children within your group as you go about this activity.

Comments

Talk with the children about how certain children may choose the same body part for the same or different reasons. You can explore how people often share ideas with others and how developing a shared vision helps them get along together. You could apply this method to generating or revisiting your group's code of conduct.

Seeking similarities

This game focuses on pooling resources in order to be effective.

Resources

A photocopy (or printout) of page 136, cut up into the separate boxes. You could laminate the sheet before cutting it to make it more durable. Before cutting, decide how many sentences you need for the activity. This depends on the number of pairs in your group. You may not need the full amount or you may need to photocopy the page and use repeats.

What to do

Explain to the children that they will each be given half a sentence. Ask them to read their sentence half to themselves. You could assist any who need help, or they could ask a friend for help. Once they have read their half sentence, the children must mingle and find the child with the other half of the sentence. When they think they have found the right person, they must check that the sentence halves they have combined make sense. After a few minutes, call the children into a circle. You may find that you have some children who have not found a partner. If so, ask them to sit near you in the circle. Then ask the children to read out their sentence parts. Get the pairs to read out the sentences that they have created, one at a time. If some of the sentences do not sound right, ask the children to sort out what went wrong. This will perhaps involve some swapping with any child who did not find a partner. Tell the children that people are often more effective if they combine resources. Ask the children if they can think of any examples of that, such as a composer and a musician – one creates the music that the other brings to life.

Comments

You could play the game again, this time asking the children to create the sentence that sounds the most bizarre.

Going undercover

This game is an enjoyable way to focus on the uniqueness of each child.

Resources

A large piece of cloth or a blanket, a source of lively music, for example *Mission Impossible* theme tune

What to do

Start the music to dance along to. Tell the children that when the music stops, they should crouch down and close their eyes. Cover one of the children with the cloth. Ask the other children to stand up and open their eyes. Get them to put questions to the covered child in order to guess their identity. These questions can be aimed at discovering who the child is (e.g. 'Do you wear glasses?') or just a way of getting the child to speak so their voice is heard. The child answering can disguise their voice to try to delay their discovery by the other children.

Comments

Ask the children how they guessed the hidden child's identity. Was it voice recognition or the answers to their questions that helped the most?

One of us

This game reinforces the idea that, although each person is unique, they share characteristics with others and belong to various groups.

Resources

None.

What to do

Ask the children to sit in a circle. Call out a category, followed by an instruction – for example:

- Everyone who has one sister, stand up, turn around and sit down again.
- Everyone who has two brothers, swap places.
- Everyone who has a pet rabbit, jump up and down twice.
- Everyone who has curly hair, shake hands with the person on your left.
- Everyone who likes carrots, run round the outside of the circle and back to your place.

Talk to the children about how they might have belonged to several categories with various children, even though they are each unique. Discuss what different groups they might belong to in life – for example, after-school clubs, blood groups, religious groups and hobby groups.

Comments

Add more fun to this game by allowing the children to think up the categories and instructions themselves.

Great gifts

This game underlines the fact that every person has something of value to offer others.

Resources

None.

What to do

Put the children into groups of four to six and ask them to decide among themselves on something each child is good at. Here are examples:

- Good at speaking in front of others.
- Good at running.
- Good at thinking creatively.
- Good at tidying up.
- Good at being quiet and creating a nice calm atmosphere.
- Good at being friendly.
- Good at being funny.
- Good at art.
- Good at being kind to animals.
- Good at writing neatly.

When the children have done this, call them into a circle and let each group state what their members are good at. This could be done through a spokesperson, who introduces each child by name and says what they do especially well; or each child could say what their own gift is. The groups could elect a spokesperson to 'sell' their group by stating how marvellous it is, naming all the skills it has to offer.

Comments

When selecting the groups, try to choose combinations so that children who lack confidence will be in a group containing someone who will help them find a personal quality. Also, if you know you have any children who will claim to be good at nothing, think of something to suggest to them before the session. You could do this indirectly by praising them for the quality you had in mind earlier in the day. You can then refer back to this should the child not be able to think of anything during the game.

Further activities

We are good at ...

Make a wall display with a caption for each child, stating 'I am good at ...'. You could include a photo of each child.

Fives

Put the children into pairs. Ask them to think of and write down five things that they have in common, for example:
   We each:

- have a brother
- have blue eyes
- support the same football team
- enjoy drawing

Ask each pair to repeat the process, this time noting five things that are different about them.

What is special to me

Ask each child to bring from home an object that has special value to them, or a photograph of themselves with their special object. Make a display of these items on a special table. You could take digital photographs of any objects brought in so that they do not need to be kept at school. If you display actual items, you may want to limit access to the table to avoid loss or damage.

4 Personal Strength

Good behaviour depends on children learning that they are able to manage their emotions and that we all need to accept responsibility for the consequences of our thoughts and actions. In other words, we all need to develop what is known as our inner locus of control. We achieve an inner locus of control when we realise that we are in charge of our own emotional life and that we can take the credit for our successes, as well as the ownership of our mistakes. Then life doesn't just happen to us any more: we have learned that life is a two-way thing and that we can have an impact on our own life story. The games and activities in this section focus on the strong emotions that we all need to learn to control, and on the concept of inner and outer strength. The overall aim is to help children recognise powerful emotions as they rise up in themselves. By doing this they can take charge of where their anger is taking them and begin to see that inner strength is of great value to them.

Back from the brink

This game explores how anger can be dissolved by an act of will if someone really wants to avoid conflict.

Resources

None.

What to do

Ask the children to spread out, stand still and close their eyes. Ask them to think of something that has made them feel angry in the past: it could be when they were unfairly told off, when someone took something that belonged to them or when a friend was mean to them. Ask them to imagine their anger as a red, hot lump in the middle of their bodies. Tell them to feel the intense heat and think that they will erupt if they do not do something. Now ask them to feel cool, soft snow drifting down onto their heads. The snow sinks into their bodies and begins to cool down the burning anger. Gradually, bit by bit, the snow extinguishes the red, hot lump. Ask the children to feel the intense pressure and heat inside their bodies slowly dispel until it has gone completely and they are back to normal. Talk to the children about why it is advantageous to find a way of getting rid of the anger we feel.

Comments

Ask the children if they think that they would be able to use this method to reduce angry feelings before they react violently towards others. You could brainstorm other strategies that they have found useful and explain that they can build up a resource bank within themselves that they can draw on in times of need. Examples could be sit quietly, go for a walk, talk to a friend, punch a pillow, count to 10 and so on.

There's a storm brewing

This game introduces the theme of strength to the children by looking at the power of nature.

Resources

None.

What to do

Tell the children to stand in a line facing you. Explain to them that they are going to act out a storm. As you introduce each element of the storm, they need to act as follows:

- A gentle wind picks up and slowly grows in strength – *the children make moaning noises like the wind.*
- Then the rain begins – *the children gently tap their fingers on their knees.*
- The rain becomes heavier – *the children stamp their feet.*
- A bolt of lightning strikes – *beginning at one end of the line, each child reacts with a start as if shocked.*
- Then there was thunder – *a single loud clap.*

The children can repeat the lightning and thunder several times as you repeat these sentences. Then talk them through the storm subsiding: the rain lessens and the wind dies down. No actions are required for this. At the end, spend a few minutes focusing on slow, deep, controlled breathing to make sure that the children are calm. Talk the children through this process. When it is complete, discuss the destructive power of storms and link this force of nature with the destructive power people have when in a temper.

Comments

Introduce the idea that it is better for people to avoid stormy outbursts, using the strategies explored on page 39, than to try to repair the damage caused to relationships by outbreaks of anger.

Volcanoes

This game focuses on how anger can build up inside people until it erupts in a violent outburst.

Resources

None. You need enough space for the children to spread out.

What to do

Put the children into groups of up to six. Ask each group to crouch down in a circle with their hands on the floor in the middle of the circle. Tell them they are going to pretend to be a volcano. They must imagine the boiling pressure of the lava building inside, slowly increasing in intensity. The children can move their arms to and fro in their circles to signify this bubbling pressure. Explain that when the pressure has increased to the point where the lava can no longer be contained, they are to jump up together and throw their arms back to mimic a volcano erupting. They could let out a loud explosive exclamation to indicate the eruption. Give the signal for them to do that yourself. At the end of the activity, spend a couple of minutes calming the children with slow, controlled, guided breathing.

Talk to the children about how pressure can build up inside people too. Ask them to suggest emotions that can cause this sort of buildup. Ask them what the worst consequences of volcanic eruptions are. An example is the damage and destruction they cause. Ask the children what kind of damage and destruction are caused by erupting tempers. If children share actual experiences, you may want to ask them to do so without naming others involved.

Comments

Encourage the children to try to feel the intensity of the increasing pressure inside their bodies as they take part in this game. It might help if they close their eyes. Also, encourage them not to erupt too quickly as the waiting will increase the pressure they feel.

That drives me so wild!

This activity focuses attention on anger and its causes.

Resources

A talking object such as a painted wooden egg.

What to do

Gather the children in a standing circle. Read this poem:

> *That makes me so angry, that makes me so mad* (shake clenched fists)
> *I've lost my happy feelings and ended up quite sad* (wipe tears from cheeks)
> *That makes me so uptight, I'm about to burst* (puff out cheeks)
> *I stamp my feet and wave my arms, it really is the worst* (stamp feet and wave arms)
> *I'm trying to be calmer; my angry mood is going* (shake arms in relaxed manner)
> *That horrid temper's on its way, my true self is showing* (wave warmly at others)

Re-read the poem, demonstrating the actions linked to each line. Repeat, this time with the children joining in. Ask them to sit down. Give one child the speaking object. Ask them to complete the sentence stem: 'One thing that makes me angry is …'. They pass the object to the person on their left. They can choose not to speak, but encourage everyone to participate. You may want to ask them not to use names. Continue until everyone has had a go. Finish on a positive note by passing a handshake round the circle.

Comments

Talk about why some children become angry about a given situation while others don't. Explore how being aware of people's sensitivities is an important skill to have.

Anger rating

In this activity the children can judge their reactions to given situations and compare their anger ratings with each other.

Resources

A photocopy (or printout) of page 137 and a pencil for each child. Five sheets of paper numbered 1-5.

What to do

Give each child a photocopy of page 137 and a pencil. Ask them to rate their anger on a scale of 1-5 in response to each item you read out: 1 is not at all angry and 5 is furious. Explain that they should circle the number they select. Read the list out, giving them time to choose the relevant number. When finished, call the children into a circle and compare how they felt about each item. Space out the numbered sheets inside the circle. Read out the first item and ask the children to stand by the number corresponding to the one they ringed. Once they have found their number, you can discuss the range of responses. Repeat for the other items.

You could explore such questions as the following:

- Were there any items that made everyone furious?
- How many 5s/1s did you have on your sheet?

Look at ways of reducing anger by using the following sentence stem 'Would it help if …?' Pretend to be angry about something. The children sit in a circle, using the sentence stem in turn to offer you strategies to help. You could also use the question 'Did you associate other feelings with any scenarios?' to explore other strong feelings they have experienced.

Comments

Make sure that the children are well spaced out when they fill in their forms. Ask them to do this in silence.

I need some space!

This is a good game to lead into a discussion about the benefits of avoiding conflict.

Resources

None. You will need plenty of room to play this game.

What to do

Ask the children to spread out around the play area. Tell them to walk around the space with their elbows sticking out, shouting, 'I need some space!' They could do this as a chant to give some form to the words. The object of the game is to avoid contact with the other children. Children who do touch each other are both out and must sit at the side of the room and watch. The game ends when it becomes too easy for the remaining children to avoid each other. Alternatively, you could decrease the space available as the number of children falls so that the level of difficulty does not decrease.

Talk to the children about the possible outcomes of this game. Explain if necessary that if the children had been allowed to barge into one another, that might have led to conflict, injury or hurt feelings. Ask the children what skills they needed to avoid one another. Use this opening to lead into a discussion on the benefits of avoiding conflict when possible.

Comments

You may need to impress upon the children that the aim of the game is to manoeuvre around each other skilfully and that they need to concentrate very hard to achieve this. You can ask the children to walk faster to make the game more difficult.

Sleeping giant

This is an exciting game that can be used to introduce a discussion about avoiding making people angry by lack of thought.

Resources

None.

What to do

The children sit in a large circle. A child is chosen to be the sleeping giant and crouches in the centre of the circle. Ask the children to move about in the space as they are quite safe while the giant is asleep. Explain that when the giant awakes, they must return to their places and sit absolutely still. The giant can catch any children who do not make it back to their space in time by touching them on their back. They are then out. Any child who moves in their seat is also out. Any child who is out must sit outside the circle. After having a good look round, the giant returns to sleep in the centre of the circle and the action is repeated. Allow a giant to have three or four goes before choosing another giant to replace them.

Talk with the children about how they kept still so as not to provoke the giant. Discuss how in life we must take care not to provoke other people to anger by being unkind to them, and not to provoke them on purpose as there might be unpleasant consequences.

Comments

It is a good idea to introduce the idea of mutual culpability when a child responds angrily to being provoked by others. You could explore ways in which a child could go for help so that they do not feel trapped in such a situation.

Body and mind

This activity looks at the requirements for both a strong body and inner strength.

Resources

A large sheet of paper, or several pieces stuck together, and a thick marker pen.

What to do

Draw two small circles on the sheet. In one write 'outer strength' and in the other 'inner strength'. Explain that you are going to make two web diagrams detailing what is linked to each. Tell the children to move around, sensing their physical strength. Ask them to repeat this, this time being aware of their inner strength.

Call the children back and create a circle with the sheet of paper in the middle. Draw radiating lines from the circle and ask them to say what came to mind when thinking about outer strength. This could include strong muscles, flexible limbs and so on. You could ask them to suggest things achieved with such attributes, such as lifting a heavy box, joining in different sports and so on. Repeat the discussion, changing the theme to 'inner strength'. Inner strength might include confidence, self-esteem, feeling valued, feeling safe, patience and so on. Put the children into small groups of up to five, depending on the size and age of the whole group, and ask them to think of ways to develop outer and inner strength. Call the children back to the circle to tell one another what they thought of. Outer strength could include items such as diet, aspects of a healthy lifestyle and sleep. Inner strength could include Circle Time, Personal, Social, Health and Economic (PSHE) activities, using calming strategies, working hard at a school and being a good friend.

Comments

Display the web diagrams on the wall for a week or two for the children to study and think through.

So strong

This activity continues the theme of exploring the power of inner strength.

Resources

Find several photos of people who are physically strong. These should include images of both male and female weightlifters, body builders or gymnasts. Collect a similar amount of photos of people who exhibit inner strength. These could include such well-known people as Gretha Thunberg, Malala Yousafzai, Dalai Lama, Marcus Rashford, Simone Biles and Emma Watson.

What to do

Show the photos to the children, one at a time. Show them the physically strong images first. Ask them to comment on each in turn and explore any shared themes. Younger children might like to stand up, flex their muscles and pretend that they are big and strong too. Show them the picture of one of the people who exhibits inner strength and ask them if they know anything about this person. Explain a little about the person's background if necessary. Ask them in what way they think this person is strong. Talk briefly about what the person achieved through their inner strength. For example, explore how Gandhi's peaceful protests brought change to his entire country. Repeat this for any other images you have for inner strength. Talk to the children about the powerful influence of inner strength and the impact that it can have on world events.

Comments

Perhaps the children could research other famous people with inner strength who made an impact on the world: for example, Florence Nightingale, Terry Waite and Elizabeth Fry.

Step this way

This game helps children to understand that a person's mood is conveyed by their body language and that we can read another person's state of mind by making use of this form of communication.

Resources

None.

What to do

Ask the children to sit in a large circle. Ask for a volunteer and tell them to walk around the circle pretending to be angry. Tell the child that they need to portray the anger in their facial expression and the way that they walk. In order to do this successfully, they need to try to conjure up the feeling of anger inside them, perhaps by thinking of something that makes – or has made – them angry. When a child has demonstrated this, ask different children to mime other emotional states, such as being sad, frightened, calm, excited, anxious and so on. Talk to the children about how our posture and movements may change with the moods that we experience.

Comments

If you have a large enough space, let half the group act out moving in a sequence of feelings that you call out. The other half of the group can observe. After a couple of minutes, swap the groups over. When both groups have had a go, bring them back to a circle and ask for observations on how they saw people's bodies change as you called out different emotions.

De-role your children – ask them to sit on their chairs and close their eyes (some children may ask if they can have some of your eye masks as they find it difficult to keep their eyes closed). Imagine it's a lovely warm day and you can feel the sun on top of your head. The sun is coming through your head and it makes your scalp tingle. As the sun comes slowly down your head it melts all your worries and your tensions, the sun even loosens your jaw so it opens slightly. The gold light goes down each vertebra of your neck and loosens any stress. It slowly comes down through your body making your heart golden and happy. As it comes down each vertebra of your spine you can feel yourself relaxing into your chair. The light gold moves through you, slowly up to your knees. Slowly, slowly down your calves of your legs into your heels and out through your toes. You feel warm and soft and happy. You know that whenever you need to get calm again you can bring an imaginary sun through your body to melt all your worries.

Walk tall

This game looks at how inner strength can affect a person's posture and convey confidence to others.

Resources

Flipchart and marker pen.

What to do

Ask the children to form a circle. Use the following script:

> *You are feeling wonderful today. You got up early, and the sun was out. You had a lovely, relaxed breakfast and, when you arrived at school, everyone was pleased to see you. You are feeling confident because you know that you are going to do your best and because you intend to concentrate and work hard.*

Tell the children to stand up really straight and tall with their heads held high, feeling the confidence and happiness of the person in the story they have just heard. Ask them to walk around the space with confidence, looking at other children pleasantly, with a smile or nodding a greeting. After a couple of minutes, call the children back into the circle. Ask them how it felt to walk round like this. Discuss the distinction between confidence and arrogance. Tell the children that inner qualities give people confidence.

Comments

Talk to the children about ways in which they could boost their inner strength. These should tie in with your school's policy on social and emotional literacy and PSHE. Brainstorm ideas with the children and write them down. Display a list of them. The list could act as a reference point for subsequent activities that cover such areas.

Further activities

When I'm cross

Ask the children to complete the sentence stem 'When I'm cross, I ...'. Their responses might include both positive and negative outcomes. Discuss some of the comments to see if their impact will be constructive or destructive.

Breathing exercises

Practise a breathing exercise, such as the following:

> *Breathe deeply and steadily in through your nose, and out through your mouth. Try to make each breath out twice as long as a breath in. To help with this, count slowly 'one' as you breathe in and 'two, three' as you breathe out. Relax your shoulders when you breathe. With each breath out, relax your shoulders until you are mainly using your diaphragm to breathe.*

Anger management techniques

Compile a list of anger management techniques with the children – for example, count to 10, deep breathing, walk away. Display them in the classroom. Role play situations to practise the techniques.

Boost your inner strength

Discuss with each child one thing they could do to boost their inner strength. This could be learning to manage a particular emotion, improving a skill such as speaking in class, having a class responsibility and so on. Make sure their suggestions are realistic. Make a record of their intention for reference. Discuss with each child how they are going to try to improve the area they have chosen. Try to elicit the strategies from them. Set a timescale to achieve the target, say half a term. You could have a celebratory 'We have boosted our inner strengths' Circle Time at the end of the term, in which children tell of their achievements.

Calm corner

Every class needs a designated calm space. Teachers are fabulously imaginative and sometimes drape silk curtains around it so it is gauzy and floaty – we can see the child is safely in there, yet they have some privacy. It should be a very sensory place. Maybe some plastic pots of herbs that they can rub, lots of different textures to stroke, a music player with nature sounds that they can put on, stories with beautiful pictures of nature in and maybe some fruit cut up that they can choose to eat or smell.

5 Strength in Numbers

Being a valued member of a group and feeling loyalty to that group encourages good behaviour in children. The games in this section look at the value of working with others to pool resources and increase effectiveness. The children examine how they can bring personal strengths to the group and how other group members can provide encouragement and the impetus to succeed.

Step in time

This game encourages children to learn that success often requires co-operation and concentration.

Resources

None. You need plenty of space for the children to move around in.

What to do

Put the children into groups of up to four, evenly matched in height if possible. Ask each group to form their own line, one behind the other and facing forwards. Ask each child to grasp the waist of the child in front of them with their arms outstretched. Tell the children that they are going to practise marching in unison by each putting their right leg forward together and then each putting their left leg forward together. Give the groups several minutes to practise this, avoiding the other groups as they do so, and then ask each group to demonstrate how well they have done.

Call the children into a circle and ask them what they found most difficult about the activity. How did they organise starting at the same time and knowing which leg to put forward first? What sort of signals did they use? Did one person lead the others? Were the other players happy to follow this leadership? How did they sort out any squabbles? Talk to the children about how success in group work depends on co-operation and all members making an equal effort.

Comments

You can add to the fun of this game by asking the children to try jumping, five-legged running or hopping together across the space in unison.

Synchronised sequences

In this game the children have to work together to match their movements. This game requires great concentration and good watching skills.

Resources

None. You need sufficient space for the groups to work in.

What to do

Put the children into groups of up to six. Tell them that their challenge is to work together to synchronise their movements. Ask each group to choose a leader and to work out a system for passing on instructions: this could be a spoken or visual sign. The group then decides on a sequence of movements; for example, stand up, sit down, cross your ankles, fold your arms, touch your face. They then need to practise this sequence so that they can reproduce it in as little time as possible. The leader could announce each action before the group do it or give a nod of the head for the next action in the sequence to be performed.

Give the groups ten minutes to practise their sequences, and then call the groups together. Ask each group to demonstrate their sequence to see which can produce the most synchronised movements. After all the groups have shown their work, number each group and ask each child to vote for the group they thought was most synchronised – other than their own. Ask the children to form a circle and discuss how they tackled this activity. What problems did they encounter and what solutions did they find?

Comments

Try the game again, and let each child take a turn at leading their group, changing the sequence each time. Discuss whether or not they enjoyed this role and why. Ask what the most difficult aspect of leading the group was.

Tuned in

In this game the children focus on using listening skills to work together.

Resources

None. Plenty of space to play in is needed.

What to do

Divide the children into two groups. You will need to keep a note of who is in each group. Give each group a sound or a simple tune, such as a nursery rhyme, to hum. Mix the children up so that they are no longer in their groups. Pick two children from each of the groups and tell the other children to mill around, making their sound or humming their tune. Ask the two children from each group to locate the other members of their group by the noise that they are making. As they find their other group members, they should direct them to one end of the room. Once the groups have all their members, ask all the children to form a circle. Discuss how they felt the activity went. Did any children have difficulty with their sound or tune? If so, when and why?

Comments

You could use this game to discuss outside influences by varying the size of the groups. The smaller group will find it more difficult to be heard against the noise of the larger group.

What would you do?

The children discuss solutions to problems and consider the consequences of actions.

Resources

A photocopy (or printout) of page 138, nine index cards and a pencil for each group.

What to do

Divide the children into groups of up to six and give each group a photocopy of page 138. Read through the scenarios on the sheet with the entire group. Tell the groups to spread out and discuss the scenarios. Ask them to come up with peaceful and effective solutions to each of them. Ask one child in each group to write or draw their group's solution for each scenario on a separate index card. Allow about 20 minutes for this. When they have finished, call the groups into a circle. Ask one child from each group to say what their group's solution to each problem was. Any group that has the same solution as one that is read out can hold up their relevant index card and say 'snap'. Repeat, with a different child presenting each solution.

Comments

You could discuss the negative developments that might follow some of the groups' suggested situations and what the consequences of these would be.

The call of the wild

This is a noisy game in which children actively seek out other group members.

Resources

You will need animal pictures – such as cats, dogs, cows, ducks, sheep – in sets of four. All the animals should have distinctive calls. For older children, you can write the names of the animals onto cards.

What to do

Shuffle the cards and give one out to each child, face down. Tell the children to have a quick look at their card, but not to let anyone else see it. Collect the cards in. Tell the children that on the count of three, you want them to walk round the room making the call of the animal that was on their card. They must listen carefully to the sounds and find the three other members of their group. Once their group is complete, they sit down together. The children must not say what animal they are. When all the groups are complete, give out the cards again and repeat the process.

Comments

With younger children, it might be a good idea to go through the animals included and practise their calls so that the children know what noise to make. If you think that they will forget their animals, they can hold onto their cards while they play the game, as long as they keep them hidden from the other children.

If the number of children is not exactly divisible by four, you will need to be watchful for groups that will have fewer than four in them, briefing them to sit down when all the members have identified one another.

Agreeing as a group

In this game, the children need to practise the skills of compromise and co-operation.

Resources

A flipchart and a marker pen, and a sheet of paper and a pencil for each child.

What to do

Put the children into groups of four. Write various categories on the flipchart, such as *lunch*, *pop star*, *television programme*, *pop song*, *Disney character*, *pet* and *wild animal*. Ask each child to write or draw something on their sheet of paper that they like from each category. Then ask each group to agree on something for each category that they all like. Tell the groups that no pressure must be exerted to try to persuade someone to agree to something that they do not like. They must discuss each item in turn and find ways to compromise and agree on their decision. Allow ten minutes or so for the groups to do this, then ask them to form a circle.

Ask how many of the categories each group has completed. If a group has not done many, ask them what problems they encountered. Ask the children what was needed of them to complete this task successfully (co-operation and a willingness to compromise in order to achieve an outcome). End the session by listening to some or all of the group choices, depending on the time that you have left.

Comments

Before the game, talk to the children about how they should behave in this activity. There should be no put-downs about other children's opinions – everyone is entitled to their own opinion. Explore the basis of good turn-taking: listening carefully, responding in a nonjudgemental way, putting aside one's own opinions and reaching a compromise.

A roll of the dice

This is an exciting game in which the competitive element encourages children to be fully cooperative.

Resources

A large foam floor dice. Sufficient room to move around is needed.

What to do

Divide the children into two groups and ask each group to sit at opposite ends of the floor space. Tell the children that you will roll the dice. When you call out the number shown, each group must organise itself into smaller units reflecting the number shown on the dice. It does not matter if some children are left over. As soon as a large group has formed as many smaller units as possible, they sit down, including any spare group members. The first large group to complete the task gains a point. Play the game a number of times.

Children can help the whole group, not just by joining in a number of children quickly but when they realise that the number is not the number being called by the teacher, they slip out of the group. Discuss with the children that sometimes we have to absent ourselves to help the majority.

Comments

When you put the children into their initial groups, try to match them evenly in terms of their skills so that one team is not significantly better at organising themselves than the other. If you want to make the game more difficult, let the two groups intermingle. Explain that they must make up the smaller groups from their own group members, so they must remember all their members. You could give each group member a piece of card of the same colour to help this process.

On cue

This game is great for cooperative group work and concentration.

Resources

A number of copies of the words of the following songs: 'One Man Went to Mow', 'Ten Green Bottles', 'This Old Man'. These should be available in your Key Stage 1 music resources, or can be found on the Internet.

What to do

Beforehand, choose a different cue word for each of the songs; for example, for 'Ten Green Bottles' you could use 'bottles' or 'wall'. Put the children into groups of up to six and space the groups out. Give each group a copy of the words of one of the songs and whisper the cue word to one child in the group. Tell the groups to get into a close huddle and ask the child whom you spoke to in each group to tell their other group members the cue they were given. Ask each group to work out a small gesture quietly, such as sniffing, touching their chin, folding their arms – it should be quite subtle and not too obvious. Explain to the children that each group will perform their song, and during it a different member of the group will perform their chosen action each time their cue word is spoken. The other groups will watch and try to guess the cue word and the action. Give the children a minute or two to decide on the order in which their players will respond to the cue word. Let each group in turn perform their song, while you read the words. After a group has performed, ask the other groups what they thought the cue word and action were.

Comments

Warn the children to whisper in their groups when they are deciding on their action, so that the other children do not hear their discussions.

Legs eleven

This is a fun game to encourage co-operation and concentration.

Resources

None.

What to do

Ask the children to stand in groups of six. Explain that you will call out a number. Each group is to work out quickly how to make this number by putting their feet on the floor. The children must not use chairs or sit on the floor. For example, if you call out 'eleven', one child in each group will have to stand on one foot. If you call out 'five', five children will have to stand on one foot and one child will have to be held off the floor. The first group with the correct number of feet on the floor gets a point.

Comments

You need to think through the numbers that you are going to use beforehand to make sure that they are possible and can be safely executed. You could play this game with the groups on PE mats to give more protection in case someone loses their balance.

Talk to the children after the game about their need to support one another in order to keep their balance. Explain that they can support one another in areas of school life that involve co-operation.

Riddle-me-ree

A good game to encourage children to use their thinking skills.

Resources

A flipchart and marker pen; a pencil and some paper for each group.

What to do

Write the following riddle on the flipchart. The letters produced spell 'thinking skills' when rearranged.

First word
This letter is in *hive* but not in *five*.
This letter looks like a railway tunnel.
You see through this letter.
This drink sounds like a letter.
This letter is in *take* but not in *tame*.
This letter is in *good* but not in *hood*.
This letter is in *need* but not in *heed*.
You use this word to describe yourself.

Second word
These three letters are the opposite of feeling well.
This letter is in *case* but not in *came*.
This letter is in *took* but not in *tool*.
This letter is in *sale* but not in *male*.

Put the children into mixed-ability groups of five or six. Explain that each line of the riddle will give a letter or letters, and that they need to rearrange them to make two words. Give the groups ten minutes to work out the problem, then sit down as a group. When the time is up or all the groups have finished, work out the riddle with them. Each group can check their own work.

Comments

Groups could work out their own riddles for other groups to solve.

Further activities

Paired riddles

Let the children work in pairs to produce riddles based on spotting a letter in one word only of a pair. These letters are used to work out a mystery word. For example, for 'cat' you could have: 'My first is in *car*, but not in *bar*; My second is in *hat*, but not in *hut*; My third is in *tin*, but not in *pin*; What am I?'

Coordinate pictures

Put the children into mixed-ability pairs and give them some squared paper. Ask a scribe in each pair to draw numbered X and Y axes from the left-hand corner. Ask the groups to devise a simple design or picture on their grid using the coordinate points as a guide, then find another pair to share their work with. Each pair in turn reads out their coordinates to the other pair, who try to reproduce the design on a fresh piece of squared paper that they draw the axes on. If they encounter problems, they should work as a group of four to try to find where things have gone wrong. Reverse the roles of the pairs and repeat.

Group quiz

Put the children into small mixed-ability groups for a quiz and give each group a pencil and some paper. Ask them to write down items in certain categories that begin with a specific letter (e.g. famous people whose forename or surname begins with the letter M; animals beginning with the letter B).

Group pictures

Put the children into groups. Give each differently coloured pieces of paper, plastic shapes (circle, triangle and square), scissors and pencils. Ask each group to draw round and cut out ten circles, ten triangles and ten squares, then make a picture with their shapes.

They could add detail using the pencils.

6 Learning to Listen

If a child is fully engaged in what is going on, there is less likelihood of inappropriate behaviour. Some children find it very difficult to listen to what the teacher is saying because their attention wanders constantly. The games in this section require the children to listen very carefully and concentrate on the action in order to participate.

Follow me

This game teaches children the benefits of co-operation and concentration.

Resources

None. You need a clear space for the children to play in.

What to do

The children move round the space in silence. Choose one child to be the leader. This child walks about with the others, and without stopping whispers to another child whom they pass, 'Follow me.' This child falls into step behind the first child. The action continues, with the leading child whispering to individual children in the same way, who then quietly join the growing line. The object of the game is for all the children to join the line, one at a time, without any hesitation and without the moving line having to stop. The line of children must move together at all times.

Comments

Remind the children that they must remain completely silent throughout this game, and that the leader can only whisper.

Behind your back

This is an effective game for keeping children's attention focused, as they have to be vigilant throughout the action.

Resources

None.

What to do

The children sit in a circle. One child is chosen to stand in the centre of the circle. This child turns round constantly, looking for any movement by the seated children. The seated children have to try to move when they think that the child in the centre has their back turned to them. If the child in the centre sees someone move, that person is out and must stand outside the circle. The game ends after an agreed amount of time or when only one child is left in the circle. The child in the centre can turn slowly or quickly to keep the seated children vigilant.

Comments

If you find that the game is taking too long, try it with two children in the centre of the circle.

This way or that way?

This game requires concentration, and the pace can be increased to make it even more absorbing.

Resources

None.

What to do

Everyone sits in a circle. Choose a child to lead the game. This child taps their right knee. The child on their right follows suit and the action travels round the circle in an anti-clockwise direction. The child leading the game can change the action by tapping their left knee when it is their turn again, which cancels the first action and begins a clockwise one with the person on their left. If the leader taps both knees, actions travel round the circle in both directions.

Comments

The children on either side of the leader of this game need to concentrate especially hard. You might want to keep the rounds of this game short to start with, so that you can change the leader regularly. If the children can cope easily with this level of the game, raise the difficulty by increasing the pace of the action or having two leaders giving instructions.

That's my cue

The children need to remain quiet and concentrate in this game as they listen for their cue.

Resources

A selection of percussion instruments: for example, maracas, egg shakers, castanets, tambourines and drums

What to do

Demonstrate how each instrument sounds, naming each instrument as you do so. Demonstrate them again in turn, asking the children what each instrument is called after you have played it. Ask the children to lie down, shut their eyes and pretend to be asleep. Choose one of the instruments as your cue instrument. Tell the children the name of this instrument. Play each of the instruments in turn. The children must listen for the cue instrument to be played. They must ignore all the other instruments until they hear the cue instrument. When they hear this instrument, they are to open their eyes and sit up. Repeat this a couple of times and then choose a different instrument.

Comments

If you think that some children may deliberately wake up on the wrong sound, you can introduce a competitive element: the children are out of the game if they sit up for the wrong sound. They become your observers.

Silent but deadly

This exciting game requires silence and concentration as anticipation builds.

Resources

None.

What to do

Choose two children, one to be a press-gang member and the other to be the press-gang leader. The remaining children stand with their eyes shut in a well-spaced circle. The two chosen children stand outside the circle. The leader whispers the name of a child in the circle to the gang member. The gang member must creep up behind that child and tap them on the shoulder. If they do this successfully, that child has been press-ganged. However, if the intended victim hears the gang member approaching, they can quickly crouch down to avoid capture. The gang member scores a point for every victim successfully press-ganged. Give each pair several turns before choosing a new leader and gang member.

Comments

Take the opportunity to discuss the historical significance of pressgangs. Play this game over several weeks so that everyone gets a turn to be a gang member and leader. You could have a press-gang league table and keep a tally of the points scored by each child when they are the gang member.

Let's get quizzical

The children must listen carefully and concentrate to play this game well.

Resources

A list of 20-30 prepared questions that require a range of the following answers: *yes*, *no*, *1*, *2*, *high*, *low*, *right* and *wrong*. Suitable questions might include these:

- Do humans have green skin?
- Is Mount Everest high or low?
- Is 12 - 6 = 9 right or wrong?

The questions do not have to be difficult.

What to do

Explain to the children that you are going to ask them questions that require specific answers. These answers have to be given by actions, not words. Demonstrate to the children the various actions. For example, 'yes' might be clap twice, 'no' might be spin round on the spot, 'low' might be crouch down and touch the floor, 'high' might be stretch both arms above your head, 'right' might be three jumps on the spot, 'wrong' might be tap your knees twice.

Ask the children to stand in a circle. Remind them that they must not say the answer aloud. Read out the questions as quickly as they can respond. After the game, go through the questions and check that the children understood them so that you can modify them for next time and clear up any misunderstandings.

Comments

Older children can be put into mixed-ability groups to work out a set of questions and responses to try with the rest of the class.

Left, right

In this game, the children have to listen attentively and be ready to respond to the cue words.

Resources

The story on page 139. You need plenty of space to play this game.

What to do

Explain that while the children walk around the room, you are going to read a story to them. Every time you say the word 'right' they must make a right turn, and every time you say the word 'left' they must make a left turn. Once a turn has been completed, they must continue walking. If they encounter an obstacle and can go no further, they must walk on the spot until they hear the next cue word. Ask the children to stand well apart before the game begins, to minimise the likelihood of their blocking one another's routes. Then read the story on page 139.

Comments

Warn the children before the game begins that they must avoid bumping into each other. If they are on a collision course with someone else, they must stop short of touching and walk on the spot until they hear the next cue word.

The ski run

This is an enjoyable game that encourages children to listen and concentrate.

Resources

None. You need plenty of space to play in.

What to do

Tell the children to space themselves out, and to pretend that they are clipping their feet into a pair of skis. The children then need to stand on the spot and mime skiing actions as you describe them. They begin by using their ski poles, thrusting their arms behind them as if pushing their ski poles into the snow, to propel themselves along flat ground. Then they crouch down in a tuck position, as if travelling downhill fast. Go through this process two or three times. Next, tell the children that they are going to slalom round a series of poles. They must bend left and right in quick succession as you instruct them in order to ski round the poles. You can then direct them over some small jumps – they should go up on their tiptoes before resuming their tucked position. Finish with a big jump. To do this, they must lean forward with feet together and arms by their sides. When you tell them to land, they hold out their arms horizontally and drop onto one knee.

Comments

Ask the children if they can add to the movements with other skiing actions. You could add some freestyle tricks and jumps.

Get to the point

The children will enjoy this exciting game that requires concentration and alertness.

Resources

A large floor dice and cards numbered 1-6. Plenty of space to move around in.

What to do

Place the number cards at different points around the room. Call the children into the centre of the room. Tell them that you will say a type of movement, such as hopping, skipping, crawling, jumping, walking sideways or walking on tiptoes. You will then roll the dice. The children must move as quickly as possible, in the manner that you described, to the number displayed around the room corresponding to the number shown on the dice. The last child to arrive at the designated number is out. The other children stay where they are. The child who is out for each turn could roll the dice for the next round, after you have announced the way of moving.

Comments

With younger children, you may decide to let them all remain in the game rather than penalising the last to arrive at the number.

Think on your feet

The children will enjoy the excitement of this fast-moving game that requires concentration and quick thinking.

Resources

A set of 24 index cards, each with a letter of the alphabet on it (omit x and z), in a box, and a wooden or plastic brick. Enough space for a big circle.

What to do

Ask the children to form a circle. Go round the circle counting in lots of six, or less depending on the size of your group. Ask each child to remember the number they were given. Place the wooden or plastic brick in the centre of the circle. Explain to the children that you will call out a category, such as a flower, a cartoon character, an animal, a colour or a character from a book. You will then call a number from the sequence you used when going round the circle. Last, you will take a card with a letter on it out of the box and call out the letter chosen. The children with the chosen number have to race to the centre of the circle and try to be the first to pick up the brick. While racing for the brick, they need to be thinking of something from the named category that begins with the chosen letter from the box. The child who picks the brick up must then immediately name the item that they thought of. If they do so, they receive a point. Any hesitation once a child has picked the brick up, before naming their item, means that they do not receive a point.

Comments

Any jostling for the brick could result in the offender(s) missing their next go.

Further activities

Suits me

Give out the same number of cards of each suit from a pack of playing cards – in a class of 32 you would use cards from the ace to the 8 of each suit. Each child is given a card at random. Call out different group categories, one at a time. The children then have to try to form the groups by looking at each other's cards. Groups could be, for example, the same suit, the same number, numbers that total 10, odd numbers at one end of the room and even numbers at the other, and black and red groups.

Card race

Give out an appropriate amount of cards, as explained above. This time, call out different tasks one at a time; for example, stand up, turn around and sit down again; run around the outside of the circle in a clockwise direction to get back to your place; stand up and touch your toes; jump three times on the spot, then sit down. When you have named a task, call a number (aces counting as 1). All the children holding that card perform the task as quickly as possible. The first child to complete the task wins a point.

Variation on Simon Says

This game is played like Simon Says, but it includes a word such as 'up' that the children must ignore. If you say a sequence of actions, such as 'Touch your toes, turn around and put your hands on your shoulders', the children follow these instructions fully. However, if you say, 'Fold your arms, stand on tiptoe and look **up** at the ceiling', they must ignore the last command as it involves the word 'up'. If a child carries out an instruction with the banned word in it, they are out.

7 Nurturing Imaginative Thought

In this section, the games concentrate on developing the children's imagination. Encouraging children to be fully engaged in an activity is one way of nurturing good behaviour, and activities that promote imaginative thought in an enjoyable way will draw the children into participating in this manner.

An alien came

An opportunity for children to use their imagination.

Resources

None.

What to do

Using the tune of 'Here we Go Round the Mulberry Bush', the children sing the following words:

> *Verse 1*
> An alien came to our little house, our little house, our little house.
> An alien came to our little house and he looked like this.
> *Verse 2*
> An alien came to our little house, our little house, our little house.
> An alien came to our little house and this is what he ate.
> *Verse 3*
> An alien came to our little house, our little house, our little house.
> An alien came to our little house and this is what he said.

After verses 1 and 2, ask volunteers to describe the alien and say what he ate. After verse 3, the children can repeat a question that you give them in an alien language of their own devising.

Comments

You might like to extend this game, by asking the children to draw a picture of how they imagine the alien to look. Some children might like to compose their own verses for the group to try out.

Predictions

In this activity, the children use their knowledge of the others in the group to try to predict their answers.

Resources

A slip of paper and pencil for each child in the group – if you have a small group, you may need more than one slip of paper per child.

What to do

Ask each child to think of a question – or questions, depending on the size of your group – that relates to a personal preference and requires a *yes* or *no* answer. For example, 'Do you like baked beans?', 'Do you like to swim?', 'Do you like [a named pop star]?'

Help any child who cannot think of a question. Give each child a slip of paper. Ask them to write their question on it. Ask the children to give you their questions and form a circle, bringing their pencils with them. Shuffle the slips and place them face down in the centre. Choose a child (child A) to take the top slip. They read the question to themselves and give it to you. You read the question out to the rest of the group and give the slip back to child A, who returns to their place. They look at the person on their left (child B) and decide whether child B will answer *yes* or *no* to the question you read out. Child A must write their prediction on the back of the slip without anyone else seeing. They ask child B the question. Child B must answer honestly. Child A then reveals if the prediction is correct. Child B takes a question from the centre and a new round begins.

Comments

You could ask the children to write their questions beforehand.

Come out, timid alien

Working in pairs, the children have to use their imagination and persuasive powers to coax out a timid alien.

Resources

None.

What to do

Put the children into pairs. Tell the children that they will take it in turns to pretend to be a timid alien. They will curl up in a ball on the floor and their partner will try to coax them out with all sorts of persuasive suggestions; for example, something nice to eat, an enjoyable activity, an interesting object to show them. The child who is the timid alien must think carefully about each suggestion. As soon as they hear one that appeals to them, they must come out of their crouch. Give the children time for each to be the alien for a couple of minutes, then ask them to form a circle to discuss the activity. Ask the children how successful they were and what sort of things worked.

Comments

Ask the children what they have learnt about how to act in order to encourage others to participate. Talk to the children about how they could relate this game to real-life incidents; for example, with a very shy child or a child who is new to the class.

The lucky star

In this guided fantasy, the children are encouraged to take a positive view of something they initially see negatively.

Resources

None.

What to do

Ask the children to lie on the floor and close their eyes. Tell them to relax their bodies, starting at their heads and working down to their toes. Ask them to think about something they do not think they are good at. Ask them to think about how they feel when they have to do this. Tell them to imagine they have wished upon a star, and are now able to do this really well. Get them to imagine how they would feel if they became very good at doing the thing they think they are not very good at. Ask them to open their eyes, slowly sit up and quietly form a circle. Discuss how they felt in this guided fantasy. What feelings did they associate with being successful in the area they chose? Discuss how it is important to remember what we are good at, and the positive feelings we have about such areas, when we tackle something we are less confident about. As there are no lucky stars, discuss how it can help to devise small achievable targets in the areas we want to improve in. Talk to the children about the fact that it is sometimes difficult to improve at certain things, even though they try. Sometimes they have to accept that these areas may always be a bit tricky, but they can persevere and not become disheartened.

Comments

Talk to the children about concentrating on their positive attributes and not comparing themselves with others.

Rewards of our dreams

The children work in groups in this activity to think of imaginative, motivational rewards that they would like for good behaviour.

Resources

A piece of paper and a pencil for each group.

What to do

Put the children into groups of five or six with paper and pencils. Ask them to think of fantastic and motivating rewards they would like for good behaviour; for example, a trip to the moon, a day riding a dolphin through warm oceans, or a visit from a favourite fictional character. Ask each group to think of ten rewards and then put them into an order of preference. Appoint a scribe in each group to write their list down. When the groups have completed their lists, call them into a circle and let one person from each group read out what they have written. Discuss any similarities between the lists. Was there a clear favourite that every group thought was best? Discuss why the children think that these rewards would be effective.

Comments

Discuss the rewards available to children within school. Make a list of additional rewards that could be achievable for the class on a regular basis or on completion of a particular task. Take a vote on the favourite choice and what it should be awarded for. Work towards it together over an agreed time period. Discuss how children can devise their own rewards too. These can be of an internal nature (pride in achieving something) or a personal goal, such as a game with some friends when they have finished their homework or chores round the house.

I've got your number

This is a good game for creating different groups of children and producing a variety of views.

Resources

Thirty pieces of paper and ten pencils.

What to do

Ask the children to think of a number between 1 and 10. Tell those who chose 1-5 to go to one end of the playing area and those who chose 6-10 to go to the other. Then tell each group to subdivide into groups of odd numbers and even numbers. Appoint a scribe for each group and give them paper and a pencil. Tell the children to discuss in their group somewhere they would like to visit. Ask them to vote on a favourite. Each scribe is to write down their group's favourite and give it and their pencil to you.

Repeat the game, asking the children to think of a different number. This time ask the groups to discuss something each child would like for their birthday. They vote and record their favourite as before.

Repeat the game a third time, discussing whom each child would like to meet from the past or present. After the voting and recording for this final round, gather the pieces of paper in and ask the children to sit in a circle. Discuss the findings of the different group combinations and see if any clear favourites come out.

Comments

If you think that children are colluding over their choice of numbers to ensure that they are always in the same group, explain that by doing that they are spoiling the game.

Counting on you

This is an enjoyable competitive game to stimulate thought and team support.

Resources

A large floor dice, a flipchart and a marker pen.

What to do

Put the children into two mixed-ability teams, A and B. Write a range of categories on the flipchart; for example, colours, months, Simpson's characters, types of shop, dog breeds and makes of car. The complexity of these categories depends upon the ability and age of your group. Try to include categories that cover a broad range of themes, not all of an academic nature, so that all children can have a turn at some point. Choose a category and roll the dice. Ask if anyone in team A can think of the same number of items in the chosen category as is shown on the dice. For example, if the dice shows the number 4, they must think of four items in the chosen category. Choose a candidate from the children in team A who raise their hand to answer. Encourage children to raise their hands only if they are confident that they can answer. If the child chosen is correct, their team scores a point. If they cannot name the correct number of items, someone from the opposing team can answer and gain the point instead. Repeat the process with team B. Continue until you have tackled all the categories.

Comments

You can be judicious about picking children. For example, when a low number is shown on the dice, you could select one of the less confident children among those who raise their hand. You may need to remind children of your class or group rules before playing this game to ensure that any over-competitiveness is curbed.

School playtime

This activity is good for group discussion and is thought provoking.

Resources

None.

What to do

Put the children into groups of up to six. Tell them that they are going to imagine they are characters in a play about a school. Ask each group member to choose a character to be, and to tell the other group members why they have made that choice. When each group has agreed on characters for their group members, let them each practise saying a sentence or two in role. These should reflect the job or role the character has within the school. Call the children into a circle and ask for a few volunteers to stand and give their short speech. For example, a caretaker would say they had to make sure the building was locked at night and that the heating was working in cold weather. They can use their own voice or invent one for their character. Ask the children who are not in that child's group to try to guess what character they are.

Comments

If you would like to extend this activity, you could compare the characters that children choose to be, discussing whether there were similar characters in all the groups. If so, why were these ones chosen?

Don't destroy our school!

In this activity, children have to combine their thinking skills to produce a reasoned argument.

Resources

A sheet of paper and a pencil for each group.

What to do

Put the children into small mixed-ability groups and give each group a piece of paper and a pencil. Tell the children that the mega-rich, miserly businessman who lives next to the school wants to knock it down because it spoils his view. He has bribed most of the council, who have passed an order to say that the school will be knocked down and everyone will have to go elsewhere. The only person that the businessman listens to is his wife, who could be persuaded to talk to her husband.

The children in their groups must think of as many reasons as they can for the school to be saved. Appoint a scribe in each group to write the reasons down. After ten minutes, call the children together and let each group read out their list. You could invite a female member of staff in at this point to act as the businessman's wife and to hear the arguments to be put to her husband.

Comments

Let the children do this activity without giving any suggestions of reasons that they might record. Alternatively, you could prompt them to think of the wider implications, if they do not come up with these themselves – such as the impact on their parents, the community and so on.

Up the ladder

In this thought-provoking activity, children are asked to choose their own criteria for rewards within the classroom.

Resources

A piece of paper and a pencil for each group.

What to do

Put the children into mixed-ability groups of five or six. Explain that they are going to think of six different achievable targets that they can try to reach as a group. Appoint a scribe for each group. They need to draw a large ladder with five rungs. Once the group has chosen its six targets, they should agree on an order of difficulty for them. The scribe then writes the targets between the rungs of the ladder, the easiest target below the bottom rung and the most difficult target at the top.

Let the children try this activity without suggestions from you to begin with. Help them if they run out of ideas with suggestions such as: have a pencil ready and sharpened before each lesson, keep your table (drawer) tidy, line up quietly to go out to break, sit on the carpet quietly. After 15 minutes, call the groups into a circle and ask someone from each group to read out their targets.

Comments

The children could take the most popular targets, varying in their level of difficulty, and make a display of a class target ladder. You could vote on the targets to include if the most popular ones are not apparent. Agree a timescale for the first target so that you can review progress. You may want to explore rewards that may be linked to reaching the targets, so that you can all enjoy the pleasure that achievement brings.

Good to great

In this activity the children are asked to think about the characteristics of being 'good' and to explore people who have had a positive impact upon the world.

Resources

Enough paper and pencils for the number of groups.

What to do

Put the children into groups of three and ask them to choose a scribe and a spokesperson. Ask each group to think of a person, past or present, who they think is really good. They also need to think about why they think that person is good.

Call the children into a circle. Ask each spokesperson to name the person their group chose and explain why they chose them. This can lead to some very interesting discussions about what constitutes a 'good' person, notably that it is more than appropriate behaviour or academic achievement.

Comments

You should acknowledge the achievements of all the people mentioned by the groups where possible, unless their inclusion is highly dubious. The children could make a display of the people chosen by the groups and their attributes. They could also spend some time finding out more about the lives of these characters.

Further activities

Thought bubbles

Draw some large thought bubbles to put up on a display board. Ask each child to write or draw in one of the bubbles something that they appreciate about school.

Behaving well

Ask the children to brainstorm the elements involved in behaving well, such as sitting quietly, being helpful and working hard. Write these in bright colours on a large sheet of card. Display it prominently to form part of your group's code of conduct.

Good behaviour symbols

Ask the children to think of symbols to use to commend good behaviour, such as thumbs up or a smiley sun. Draw each of these on a card. Display a different card each week and write children's names by the symbol to commend them for good behaviour.

DIY target pictures

Ask the children to brainstorm ideas for pictures to record group targets, such as a ladder or an octopus. When you have a list with several items on it, ask each child to choose one from the list and draw it on a piece of paper. Let each child choose up to eight achievable behaviour targets to write on their picture. Some should be easy to achieve, such as pushing their chair under the table when they stand up.

Something good I have done

Pass a talking object, such as a painted egg, round the circle, and ask each child to complete the sentence stem: *'Something good I have done this week was …'*.

8 Energetic Games for Excess Energy

Using up excess energy in a controlled way is crucial to promoting better behaviour. Restless children find it hard to concentrate and remain focused on the work in hand. The games in this section are lively and engaging, ideal for promoting fun and enjoyment within the group.

Breaching the wall

This fast game requires concentration.

Resources

None. You need plenty of space for the children to play in.

What to do

Tell the children to form a wall by making a diagonal line across the room. There should be gaps between the children in the line. Choose two children to stand on opposite sides of the wall. The aim of the game is for the two children to join up on one side. They have to achieve this by trying to slip through one of the gaps in the wall. They cannot touch the wall or use force to break through it. As soon as a gap closes up, they have to try to get through somewhere else along the wall. The two children could work together, the child facing the wall keeping the children in the wall occupied while the child on the other side of the wall sneaks through a gap unnoticed. The children in the wall can move to close any gaps, but they are not allowed to hold hands. Give each pair a minute or so to try to get together before changing roles.

Comments

While this game is primarily for physical exercise, you could use it as an introduction to talking about the frustration of being prevented from doing what you want to do. Ask the children to tell you occasions when this might happen in school. Ask them to think of inappropriate ways in which people might respond to frustration; for example, losing their temper and saying unacceptable things and lashing out at others. Discuss the likely outcomes of such actions. Lead on to exploring what might be more effective responses, such as talking a problem through, negotiating a solution and remaining calm.

Chase the chair

This is a fast, active game that children really enjoy.

Resources

A circle of chairs, and enough number cards for each child to have one.

What to do

Ask the children to form a circle of chairs and to sit down. Give each child a number card and ask them to look at their number without letting anyone else see it. Tell the children to remember their number and then collect in the cards. Choose one child to begin the action. Remove their chair from the circle. They stand in the place where their chair had been previously. Explain that this child will call out two numbers from the range used in your group. The children with these numbers must try to swap places while the standing child tries to sit on one of the vacated chairs. Whoever is left without a chair stands in the gap in the circle and calls the next two numbers. The game continues in this manner.

Comments

If a caller fails to secure a chair after three attempts, choose another child from the circle to swap places with them.

Keep your head

In this game, physical activity is controlled and combined with concentration.

Resources

A beanbag for each child in the group. Space to move about in.

What to do

Tell the children that they must concentrate really hard in this game as they are going to be performing physical activities while balancing a beanbag on their head. Instruct the children in turn to walk, hop, skip and jump, while trying to keep the beanbag on top of their head without holding onto it. Gradually make the challenges more demanding, such as *Sit down and stand up*, *Turn around on the spot* and so on.

Comments

The children could do this activity in pairs or groups, timing one another to see who can keep the beanbag in place for the longest time. It might be wise to set a maximum time for this.

Bean and gone

This is a fast, competitive game that children enjoy.

Resources

Two beanbags. You need space for two circles of children.

What to do

Put the children into two teams and tell each team to form a circle. Explain that they are going to have beanbag races. In the first race, each team must pass their beanbag in front of them from child to child. As soon as it reaches the child who began the round, that child raises the beanbag in the air. In the second race, they pass the beanbag from one to another behind their backs, finishing as before.

For the third race, choose a child from each team to stand in the centre of their circle. They throw the beanbag to each child in their team in turn. If a child drops it, the child in the centre must retrieve it and throw it to that child again. If they miss it a second time, the child in the centre retrieves the beanbag and moves on to the next child in the circle. When a child does catch the beanbag, they throw it back to the child in the centre of their circle.

For the last race, each team stands in a line with their legs apart, facing forwards. The child at the front passes the beanbag through their legs to the child behind them. The beanbag continues to the end of the line. When it reaches the last person, they pass it to the person in front of them over that person's shoulder. The children continue to move the beanbag forward. The winning team is the one that gets their beanbag back to the front quickest.

Comments

Allow younger children some time to practise the different passes before they take part in a race.

Two's company

This is a fast, active game that children enjoy.

Resources

None. You will need plenty of space. This game requires an uneven number of players, so you may have to join in.

What to do

Pick one child to start the game on their own. Form the other children into pairs at random. Tell the children that you will call out ways of moving around in the space in their pairs; for example: *hopping, skipping, jumping, tiptoeing*. After a few calls, say 'All change!' When the children hear this, they must separate from their partner and find a new partner. During the changeover, the child standing out should find a partner of their own, leaving a different child to stand out for the next round. The game continues in this manner. Once a child has been touched by another child, they have to be that child's partner for the next round.

Comments

Impress on the children that if they are touched, they can't refuse to be the other child's partner.

Mixed messages

This is a good game for memory training as well as physical exercise.

Resources

None.

What to do

Put the children into pairs. Explain to them that each child in turn is going to perform an action to their partner, while saying they are doing another action. For example, they might bend down and touch their toes while saying 'I am jumping on the spot three times'. Their partner has to listen to what is said and act out the statement, while saying something different, such as 'I am clapping my hands four times'. Let the children practise a sequence in their pairs for a while, and then ask for volunteers to show the others their routine. When the children are confident about what to do, get them all to play.

Comments

The children may find the concept of this game difficult to grasp, and it may be easier to model the concept with a teaching assistant or a reliable child. Once the group understand how to play, they will quickly master the technique.

A soft-ball sandwich

This is an active game that requires concentration and co-operation between partners.

Resources

A sufficient number of large balls for one between two. Space to move around in.

What to do

Put the children into pairs of roughly equal height. Give each pair a ball, which they need to hold still. When the game begins, each pair must keep their ball sandwiched between their two hands, one child's right hand on top of the ball and the other child's left hand beneath the ball. With the ball held in this manner, they must then perform actions called out by you. The children in any pair that drops their ball are out. They must sit down and hold their ball still. Call out such actions as *Kneel down*, *On the count of three take one jump on the spot* and *Stand on one leg*. The game is over when only one pair is left or when an agreed time period is over.

Comments

You could set up obstacle courses for groups that become really proficient at this game. This game can be played purely for fun without the competitive element. A similar enjoyable game is to pass a small ball held under their chins from child to child in a line.

The mouse, the tree and the wind

In this game children have to listen carefully for cue words in a story that require certain actions.

Resources

The story on page 140 (photocopied if you wish). Plenty of space to move around in.

What to do

Explain to the children that you will read them a short story in which there are certain cue words. When they hear these words, they must perform specific actions. When they hear the word *mouse* they must crouch down; when they hear the word *tree* they must stretch up, and when they hear the word *wind* they must spin round on the spot on one foot. Read the story on page 140.

Comments

This is not as easy as it looks. Once the children get the hang of it, they could try writing their own scripts to use for this game.

At the races

The children need to concentrate and work together to be successful at this game.

Resources

None. The game is best played on grass.

What to do

Put the children into pairs. Explain to them that they are going to play the front and back legs of a horse. Like a pantomime horse, one child will stand upright and be the front legs of the horse, while their partner will stand behind them and bend over, holding the child in front at the waist, making the back legs of the horse. Give the pairs time to practise, so that each child can have a go at the different positions and each pair knows which combination works best for them. Children need to practise so that they can move well together. You could stop the activity here or, if you think that the pairs have mastered moving in this manner, you could hold races to find the champion horse (preferably outside on the grass, in case of tumbles). These could be flat races or over jumps made using low obstacles created from wooden bricks or PE equipment.

Comments

Warn the children before playing that the child in each pair who is the horse's front legs needs to take care and not run so fast that they pull their partner over.

Take your partner

In this energetic game, children have to pay attention, and think and move quickly.

Resources

A range of PE equipment depending on your choice. A large space such as the hall or outside. This game requires an even number of players, so you may have to join in.

What to do

Space out the equipment you have chosen round the playing area. Number your children so that you end up with pairs (e.g. with 30 children, number them 1-15 to make 15 pairs). Ask the children to mingle in the centre of the playing area. Call out an instruction, such as one of the following:

- Throw a ball to each other ten times.
- Collect a beanbag from one end of the area and take it to your partner at the other end, who must return it.
- Run a complete circuit of the room together.

Immediately after calling out the activity, call out two numbers. A child with either number has to quickly find another child with the same number. The other children stand still. The pair perform the activity you called out. The first pair to finish can select the next activity.

Comments

You could tell the children what equipment is available beforehand and brainstorm the tasks with them.

Further activities

Team-bending races

Set up two slalom courses with six well-spaced markers in a line. Divide the children into two teams. Ask each team to line up, a marked distance before the first marker in their course. On your command, the first child in each team runs down the line of markers, weaving in and out. They run round the end marker and weave back. When they get back, the second child can begin their turn. The first team to complete the course is the winner.

Team race

Divide the children into two to four teams. Each team has a large ball or balloon. Line the teams up at one end of the playing space. The first child in each team must move to the other end of the room and back as quickly as possible with the ball held between their legs. They must not hold the ball with their hands. The first team to complete the course is the winner.

The troll and the billy goats

Choose a child to play the troll. This child stands in the middle. The other children line up at one end of the room. These children call out: 'Troll, troll, please may we cross your bridge?' The troll replies, 'Only if you have the letter … in your name'. Any children who have the nominated letter in their name walk safely past the troll to the other end of the space. Once these children are across, the remaining children have to make a run for it. The troll tries to tag as many as possible before they reach the other side. The children who are tagged either sit out for the rest of the game or help the troll, depending on what you decide at the start. The game proceeds in this way until only one child is left. This child becomes the new troll. You could keep a list of children who have been trolls so that, over time, everyone gets a turn.

9 Games to Promote Calm

The games in this section can be used when children are restless or overexcited. Activity followed by relaxation will help to get rid of pent-up energy, so that children will be more receptive to learning.

Best foot forward

In this game the children use up their excess energy. Then the pace slows and they rest their minds and bodies.

Resources

None. You will need plenty of space to move about in.

What to do

Demonstrate how to march to the chant below. Practise saying it with them, repeating each line before you introduce the next. Once they have a sense of the rhythm, tell them to stand one behind another, all facing the same way, with sufficient space between to move freely. Take up your position at the front and lead them in a brisk march. Explain that you are going to march in time to the chant below. Chant one line and let the children repeat it before you move on to the next. Keep the pace brisk.

> *This is how we march along with our special marching song. Swing your arms each time you walk, do not chatter, do not talk. Always keep your steps in time with our easy marching rhyme.*
> *Look ahead, not left or right.*
> *Keep the one ahead in sight.*

When you think that the children are beginning to tire, gradually slow down your movements until you reach a halt.

Comments

Once the children have mastered marching together, introduce an element of unpredictability by varying your pace and speed.

Fast and slow

This is a game that follows hard physical activity with slow and calming movements to reduce restlessness.

Resources

None. Plenty of space to move about in.

What to do

Ask the children to stand in a line facing you. Explain that you are going to lead through a routine of aerobic exercises. These might include marching on the spot, jumping on the spot, star jumps, arm stretches and so on. To make it more exciting, start the actions at a moderate pace and then speed them up, changing them frequently to see how many children can keep up with you.

When the children are beginning to tire, introduce slower and more deliberate movements to create a sense of calm, such as slowly kneeling, placing your arms around your knees and your head on your arms.

Comments

This game can also be played in the classroom, with children standing near their usual place if an activity needs an injection of energy. You will need to choose your exercises with care if using this smaller space. Once children understand the movement from brisk exercise to calming actions, they could devise their own routines to share with the group.

Fighting the marshmallow

This is a great game for letting off steam and reducing pent-up aggression in the children.

Resources

A source of music and some loud dramatic music such as the '1812 Overture' by Tchaikovsky and a calmer piece such as 'Albatross' by Fleetwood Mac. You need plenty of room to move about in.

What to do

Tell the children to spread out so that they have enough space to move about in without touching anybody. Explain to the children that they are to imagine that a giant marshmallow is bearing down upon them. They have to mime trying to fight the marshmallow off. Tell the children that they need to do this on the spot and not move around the space. However, eventually, the marshmallow will overwhelm each of them. When it does, they will find that it is a surprisingly pleasant sensation. They have to mime themselves sinking contentedly into its dense, soft mass and relaxing all their limbs and their mind as they wallow in the gentle hold of the marshmallow. Tell the children that you will play two different extracts of music to accompany their actions. Play the dramatic piece as the children wrestle with the marshmallow, and switch to the calmer piece to bring the activity to a peaceful conclusion.

Comments

You might need to explain to the children that this activity is only to be played when you are around and the music is playing.

The spring has sprung

This is a good activity for releasing tension in a controlled way.

Resources

None. Sufficient space to move around freely is needed.

What to do

Tell the children to lie down on their backs and then to curl themselves up into a tight ball, holding their limbs very tense. Then talk the children through releasing their limbs from the ball, one by one. Each limb should spring out when instructed and bounce a few times in the air before coming to rest gently on the floor. Once all the limbs are released and the children's bodies are completely relaxed, reverse the process for each limb until the children are once again in tight balls. Finish the game by easing the tension by instructing the children to release each limb again.

Comments

You could try getting the children to release all their limbs at once in a huge surge of energy.

Walk the talk

This game takes children through a range of fast and slow movements to release excess energy and then to calm them.

Resources

None. You need plenty of space to move about in.

What to do

Explain to the children that you are going to call out different people to mime. They need to move in a way that reflects that person. The first people you mention should be people who move quickly. Gradually introduce people who move more slowly, so the pace decreases and eventually stops. You could try the following:

- A sprinter – run quickly.
- A marathon runner – running at a slower pace.
- A long-distance walker – a brisk walk.
- A mountaineer – laboured, slower walking.
- A tightrope walker – slow, precise steps.
- An astronaut on the moon – very slow and exaggerated movements.
- A guard outside Buckingham Palace – upright and motionless.

Once they have mastered this, you could call out the names in random order, always finishing by slowing down to a final halt. If they don't change when you call out a new action, they march on the spot until you call the next.

Comments

Let the children think up some other mimes to replace some of your choices, or provide examples of paces not included.

Don't panic!

This is an enjoyable game that has a calming effect on children.

Resources

None. You need plenty of space to move about in.

What to do

Tell the children to space themselves out in the playing area. Choose two children, one to be the 'trickster' and one to be the 'calmer'. Ask the children to walk about in a normal manner, trying to avoid the trickster. The trickster must move about quickly, tagging as many children as they can. Any children who are tagged need to walk in an unsteady and jerky manner. The calmer meanwhile tries to touch as many of the children who have been tagged as possible on the shoulder, restoring them to calm, smooth movement. Play the game for two minutes, then stop it and count how many children are still under the trickster's influence. Congratulate both the trickster and the calmer on their efforts. Choose a new trickster and calmer and play the game again.

Comments

Impress on the children that they must stop their movements as soon as the calmer touches them. You could use this game as an introduction to a discussion about ways in which children can develop their own internal calmer for difficult situations. You could explore strategies that the calmer might use, and display them for reference.

A sprinting six

This is an exciting way to release energy and dispel tension.

Resources

A whistle and a large floor dice. Plenty of space to play in.

What to do

Explain to the children that each number on the dice represents a different action. For example:

1 *pigeon steps (Small steps with inward-turning toes)*
2 *slow-motion walk*
3 *walk*
4 *jog*
5 *run*
6 *sprint*

Demonstrate any of the actions that need explanation. Explain to the children that, after the first action has been chosen, you will allow them time to carry it out before you blow the whistle. When they hear the whistle, they must come to a halt. You will then roll the dice again and call out the next number. They are to perform the related action until they hear the whistle again. The game proceeds in this manner.

Comments

The children need to be particularly careful when running and sprinting to avoid colliding with others. You may decide to have all the children moving in one direction because of this. In that case, add 'clockwise' to numbers 5 and 6.

Running water

This game explores a range of movements.

Resources

None. You need plenty of space to move around in.

What to do

Explain to the children that they are going to pretend to be various forms of water. They must move in ways that relate to the form called out. The words and related movements could be as follows:

- Rapids - *run*
- River - *walk*
- Stream - *pigeon steps*
- Ice - *stand still*

Practise calling the four words out so that the children get used to them and the movements they relate to. When you are ready to play the game, choose one child to be the water collector. This child has to try to catch other children. They can only catch children when you call 'ice', so that everyone has to stand still. At this point, the water collector is allowed to catch anybody within three steps of the collector's stopping point. Anyone caught by the collector is out. As the number of children left decreases, you can use the 'ice' command to help the collector by calling it when they are close to a number of children. Continue the game until all the children have been caught or the children begin to tire.

Comments

If a water collector has real problems with catching towards the end of the game, allow them to choose one or two additional collectors from the children already caught to help them.

The golden dome

A guided fantasy with visual prompts that are calming.

What to do

Ask the children to lie down on the floor and close their eyes. Encourage them to relax and feel comfortable. Talk the children through the following visualisation:

You are slowly floating upwards through a clear blue sky. You leave the clouds far behind you and continue rising until you find yourself travelling in outer space. You are surrounded by darkness; everything is black. You see a tiny pinprick of light in the distance and you slowly travel towards it. As you get nearer, the pinprick of light becomes the size of a 1-penny piece and then a 2-pence piece. In your mind, focus on the light and nothing else. The light grows steadily until you can see that it is a huge round hole. Light is pouring out of the hole into the surrounding darkness. You glide through the entrance to the hole. You find yourself in a tunnel full of different colours. The tunnel leads you to a huge cave. In the centre of the cave is a simple white building with a domed roof of shimmering gold. You go through the door of the building. Inside is a single room with walls painted deep red. There is a bed covered in soft red velvet in the centre of the room.

You lie down on the bed. It is very comfortable and you feel relaxed. The deep red of the walls makes you feel calm and safe and you feel very drowsy. You lie quietly on the bed, enjoying a sense of peace. Now, quietly, I want you to come back to the room, holding that peace and calmness inside to carry with you for the rest of the day.

Comments

This activity can be used before a demanding task or after an energetic activity or playtime.

Floating

A guided fantasy to encourage the children to relax.

What to do

Ask the children to lie down on the floor, close their eyes, relax and feel comfortable. Talk them through this visualisation:

You are travelling through a dense undergrowth of bushes. Under your feet, the ground is wet and muddy. You have to push your body through the thick vegetation. Pulling each of your feet out of the wet, sticky mud makes you feel like you are walking through treacle. On your back is a rucksack that is both extremely heavy and awkward to carry. Imagine the effort of each step as you push your body forwards and lift your weary legs. Your back is aching and your limbs are heavy. You feel exhausted, as if you cannot take another step. But you have to carry on. Suddenly you break through the undergrowth into a small clearing. In this clearing there is a brook of clear water. You crouch down and drink some of the water. You feel the water slipping down your dry throat. It tastes cold and refreshing. The water makes your limbs feel lighter. Your weariness vanishes. Your body starts to feel weightless. Suddenly your feet leave the ground, and you float slowly into the air. You feel a cool breeze brush against your face. You float upwards, higher and higher, until you reach a large white, fluffy cloud. You gently sink down to lie on the cloud. You feel its comforting softness and you become totally relaxed and refreshed. Now, quietly, I want you to come back to the room holding that new peace.

Comments

This activity can be used after a demanding or energetic activity.

Further activities

Choose a relaxing, gentle story to read to the children. Ask them to lie down on the floor and close their eyes. Play soothing music – such as 'In a Landscape' by John Cage or 'Pieces in a Modern Style' by William Orbit – quietly in the background while you read.

Moving symbols

Ask the children to make up some symbols for different ways of moving; for example, tense, slowly, lazily, relaxed, fast, awkwardly, energetically and gracefully. Draw each symbol on a card and use the cards to explore different movements. Ask the children to move around in the manner of the symbol on the card that you are holding up.

Be peaceful

Ask the children to lie on the floor next to one another in a long line, with their heads on the same side. Tell the children to close their eyes. Walk down the line and gently touch each child on the shoulder, saying, 'Be peaceful and calm'. This works well after a disruptive playtime.

10 Games to Promote Positive Group Dynamics

The games in this section are designed to celebrate the caring community you are building in your classroom. Building a sense of membership of this community allows each child to feel valued, grounded and safe. It also helps to minimise the kind of disruptive behaviour that has its roots in insecurity and anxiety. Earlier activities in this book have stressed the importance of inner strength and of working successfully with others to promote group strength. These games allow the children to enjoy the benefits of positive group dynamics and to take pleasure in one another's company.

The en-chanting class

This activity is an enjoyable way to promote a positive attitude in the group.

Resources

A flipchart.

What to do

Show the children the following chant, written on a flipchart:

> We're pleased to be in … class.
> We're happy to be here.
> We're all fantastic children, Let's give ourselves a cheer.
> Hip, hip, hooray!

Read the chant together and practise it a number of times. Turn the page of the flipchart over and see if the children can remember it without having the words in front of them. Once the children have mastered the rhyme, you could add a clapping beat.

Comments

Ask the children to brainstorm all the reasons why their group is fantastic. You could make a display of the statements collected.

A good word

This is an enjoyable activity to promote positive affirmation within the group.

Resources

A large, lightweight ball that bounces well.

What to do

Ask the children to stand in a large circle. Give one child the ball to start the game. Ask them to think of a positive adjective to describe their group or the work that they do, such as *caring, fun, interesting, helpful*. Once they have said their word, they carefully bounce or throw the ball to another child, before sitting down. The second child says their own chosen word and then bounces or throws the ball to another child, before they too sit down. This game continues until the final person receives the ball. They say their word and then bounce or throw the ball to you.

Comments

Before you play, stress that the children do not have to think of different words. They can repeat a word that another child has said, if they want to. You could allow younger children to roll the ball to each other.

Triangular poems

This is a good activity to encourage children to think of positive aspects associated with belonging to their group.

Resources

Enough pieces of paper and pencils for one for each group.

What to do

Put the children into mixed-ability groups of up to four, and give each group a piece of paper and a pencil. Appoint a scribe and spokesperson for each group. Ask each group to write a triangle poem about a positive aspect or aspects of belonging to their class. An example is as follows:

We

like being

in Maple class

because the children are

friendly, kind, hard-working and caring.

Give the groups 15 minutes to work on their poems, then call the children into a circle and ask the spokesperson from each group to read out their group's poem. Explain to the children that you chose a triangular shape for the poems because it has a strong base to build upon. This is how their class should be – with a strong base of good behaviour.

Comments

Cut out triangles of coloured card for the children to write their own poems on and display them round the room.

The animal questival

This is an exciting game for the children to enjoy and it encourages cooperative working.

Resources

Slips of paper, each with the name of an animal on it.

What to do

Put the children into mixed-ability groups of up to four. Give each group one of the slips of paper, and warn them not to let any of the other groups see what animal's name is on their slip. Give the children a few minutes to discuss, in whispers, how they could describe their animal without naming it. Ask them to come up with some statements to describe their animal, so that each group member has something to say. Each group needs to decide on the order to give their statements in – perhaps most difficult first – and who is going to say each of them. Let each group describe their animal in turn for the others to guess. Do not allow any guesses until all the group members have said their statements.

Comments

As a variation on this, the groups could decide on a mime that they all perform at once to describe their animal.

Top ten

This is a fast game that keeps children alert and involved.

What to do

Gather the children together in a circle. Explain that they are going to count from 1 to 10 round the circle. Choose a child to begin at 1. The child on their left says 'two' and so on. When 10 is reached, the next child begins at 1 again. Practise this a few times until the children can do it smoothly and without hesitation.

Now introduce a new element: the children must not say '5'. If a child is due to say this number, they remain quiet and the sequence continues with the child on their left saying '6'. When the children have mastered this, introduce the same rule for other numbers. You can make it more difficult by using more complex rules for exclusion, such as all odd numbers or all multiples of, for example, 2. These can vary, depending on the ability and age of the group.

Comments

If you want to make the game competitive, you can have a rule that all children who say a number incorrectly or hesitate are out.

What did I do?

This is an enjoyable guessing game that gets children thinking and working together as a team.

Resources

None.

What to do

Divide the children into two equal teams. Explain that members of each team, one at a time, can volunteer to be questioned by the other team about something exciting or enjoyable they have done recently; for example, a visit to a zoo, a game in the park and so on. Members of the opposing team try to work out what the event is by questioning the child. They can ask such questions as:

- Did you visit a special place?
- Was it a theme park?
- Was it a special celebration?
- Were you sitting down watching something?

When a child is about to be questioned, they need to whisper their event to you. You choose children from the other team to put their questions. Get them to put their hands up if they have a question. After each question, ask the questioning team if they would like to make a guess. Children should put their hand up if they want to guess. Only one guess is allowed before another question is asked. If a guess is correct, the questioning team receives a point. For two consecutive wrong guesses, a point is lost. If, after six questions, the questioning team has not reached the answer, the child being questioned reveals what they did.

Comments

Be prepared to give helpful suggestions to any child who says they have done nothing interesting; you could refer to a school event.

The enchanted forest

This is an active game for fun and enjoyment that you can use as a lead into talking about the need for care in interacting with others.

Resources

None. Plenty of space to move about in.

What to do

Choose six children, three to be elves and three to be goblins. The remaining children are trees in the enchanted forest. Explain to the children that the goblins are trying to catch the elves, who are playing in the forest. The trees space themselves out in the playing area. The elves run in and out of the trees, trying to keep away from the goblins, who are trying to tag them. If an elf is tagged by a goblin, they must move to one side of the playing area. The trees can move about the playing area and can shelter the elves from the goblins behind their bodies. After several minutes, or when all the elves are caught, stop the game and change the roles.

Comments

Stress before the game that the trees and goblins are not allowed to touch one another, so there will be no pulling, holding, pushing or barging. This game is as much about being careful around others as it is about having fun.

Colour coded

This is a fast-moving game that demands concentration if the whole group is to enjoy it.

Resources

Two sets of different-coloured PE bands or bibs, enough for the entire group in two equal teams. Plenty of space to run round in.

What to do

Divide your group into two equal teams. Give one set of coloured bands to each team to wear. Explain to the children that this is a tag game. Each child can only tag someone from the other team, wearing a different-coloured band from their own. For example, using red and blue bands, once a child wearing a red band has been tagged, they hold hands with the child who tagged them, who is wearing a blue band. They then try to tag others – the child with the red band can only tag a child with a blue band and the child with the blue band can only tag a child with a red band. The game continues like this until there are six children in a line. The sixth splits off and begins to tag on their own, so that there will be two groups chasing and tagging. Each time a line accumulates six children, the last to be tagged breaks away to begin their own line.

Comments

Stress that lines of tagged children need to co-operate in order to grow. Teams that do not co-operate could be penalised with a 30-second cool-off period on the side of the playing area. You could make this game even more complicated by using three or four different colours that have to appear in a specific sequence.

Down in the woods

This is a game that shows the fun that can be had in a group.

Resources

None. You need plenty of room to run around in.

What to do

Ask the children to stand in a circle. Choose one child to begin the game by walking round the outside of the circle in a clockwise direction while the other children say the following:

> *Down in the woods by the old oak tree,*
> [name of child] *was playing, as happy as can be. When up popped a rabbit, and said, 'You can't catch me! One, two, three!'*

When the children say the last word of the line 'You can't catch me!', the child walking round the outside of the circle taps the child nearest to them. That child (the rabbit) quickly begins to run in a clockwise direction around the outside of the circle. At the end of the line 'One, two, three!', the original child gives chase and tries to tag the rabbit before it gets back to its space in the circle. Choose a different child to begin the game again.

Comments

Keep a class record of the children who have had a turn at being the rabbit and the chaser, so that over a few weeks all the children have a turn at both roles.

It's a celebration

This activity gives children an opportunity to celebrate their efforts to behave well.

Resources

A flipchart and a marker pen.

What to do

Brainstorm with the children a list of all the advantages of good behaviour for the whole class, such as everyone is able to learn well, everyone feels more successful and happier, there is more goodwill towards each other and they are happier about coming to school. Write down all the points that they make. The resultant list could be made into a poster to display. Let the children celebrate by choosing one or two of their favourite games to play.

Comments

Advertise this session beforehand so that other classes and teachers are aware of the celebration and can congratulate your group on their good behaviour.

Further activities

Good behaviour tree

Make a large display depicting a bare tree trunk. Let the children earn first paper leaves and then paper fruit for good behaviour, to stick on the tree. When you decide that the tree looks full, reward the children with a special games session.

Incentives

Choose a different incentive display for each half-term – novelty is a great stimulator. Ideas are: a garden of flowers – children earn centres, petals, stems and leaves; and a person – children earn body parts until the figure is complete. Choose a different reward each time to celebrate class success; for example, a disco, a session of parachute games or a picnic.

Names in the hat

Put slips of paper, each with the name of a child from the group on it, into a hat. Each day pull a name out and let that child choose something for the whole class to enjoy. It could be a greeting, a Circle Time game or a song.

Wall displays

Make a feature of a prominent wall display that praises the good behaviour of your class. Change it each term to keep it fresh and attractive.

Printable Materials

The following pages can be photocopied or downloaded from https://resourcecentre.routledge.com/speechmark for printouts. Many of the resources are reused by the children. Ideally, they should be copied onto thin card or laminated.

The face fits

Copyright material from Mosley and Sonnet (2026) *101 Games for Better Behaviour*, Routledge

How would you feel?

You are opening a birthday present.

Children are laughing at your new school trousers.

The teacher has given you a 'Good work' sticker.

You have fallen over and cut your knee.

You have just broken your mum's favourite ornament.

You are going to Disneyland tomorrow.

Your friend has said something mean about you to someone else.

The teacher has told you off for something that you didn't do.

You hear a strange noise outside your door when you are in bed.

You have an important maths test tomorrow.

Your pet hamster has died.

Your friend has a new bike – you have wanted one for ages.

You have just started at a new school and don't know anybody.

You have just come back from a lovely stay at your aunt's.

You are having your favourite meal tonight.

Copyright material from Mosley and Sonnet (2026) *101 Games for Better Behaviour*, Routledge

It's not really funny

Thinking about feelings

Copyright material from Mosley and Sonnet (2026) *101 Games for Better Behaviour*, Routledge

What could you do?

Emote-ivate

angry · bored · excited · surprised

worried · happy · jealous · frightened · sad

This is me

My name is ....

I am a ....(boy/girl)

I am ....years old

My hair colour is ....

I like to eat ....

I wish I could ....

I am good at ....

I would like to go to ....

My best present would be ....

At home I like ....

My favourite lesson is ....

When I grow up, I should like to be ....

Three groups

Long, long ago, there were three groups. The first group was called Booja and they lived in the north; the second tribe, the Lallis, lived in the south; and the Widgells lived in the middle. The Boojas and the Lallis were always fighting, which was not much fun for the Widgells as either the Boojas were marching south through their land, or the Lallis were marching north through their land. The Widgells decided that they needed a plan to stop the fighting, and so they sent a message to the Boojas telling them that they would join forces with the Lallis to fight them if they marched through their land once more. This alarmed the Boojas as they knew the combined forces of the Lallis and the Widgells would defeat them. The Widgells did the same to the Lallis, who realised that they would be defeated if the Widgells joined forces with the Boojas. For a time, the arguing groups remained in their own territories and peace reigned over the land. In fact, as the Boojas, Lallis and Widgells mixed on peaceful terms they found they had more in common than they thought, and became friends.

Seeking similarities

That flower is very pretty	with its bright orange petals.
I do like ketchup	on my fish and chips.
This racehorse is really fast	and will definitely win the race.
King Henry VIII is the King who	had six wives.
Jelly is delicious	with ice cream.
Shrek is a funny film	about a green ogre.
If you clean your teeth regularly	you may not need any fillings.
When a volcano erupts	it can spit out red-hot lava.
Worms are good for gardens	because they break up the soil.
The eagle is a bird of prey	and catches animals with its sharp talons.
The bear is grumpy today	because it has a sore head.
The stars look bright tonight	and I can see the Dog Star.
The snow is deep and hard packed	so you can ski safely.
There is a huge shark	swimming in this part of the ocean.
You can see across the Houses of Parliament	from the top of the London Eye.

Copyright material from Mosley and Sonnet (2026) *101 Games for Better Behaviour*, Routledge

Anger rating

Circle a number from 1 to 5 to indicate how angry you would feel about each of the situations below.

Your television has gone wrong.	1	2	3	4	5
Your best friend has gone off with someone else.	1	2	3	4	5
The teacher tells you off unfairly.	1	2	3	4	5
Your mum makes you go to bed early.	1	2	3	4	5
You mess up a piece of work.	1	2	3	4	5
Someone pushes in front of you in a queue.	1	2	3	4	5
You have a supply teacher you really dislike.	1	2	3	4	5
You lose some homework you spent hours doing.	1	2	3	4	5
Your friends make fun of your new clothes.	1	2	3	4	5
Someone calls you a mean name.	1	2	3	4	5
Some children won't let you join in a new game.	1	2	3	4	5
Your dad makes you tidy your bedroom.	1	2	3	4	5
You have accidentally broken a new toy.	1	2	3	4	5
Your mum won't let you stay up to watch a television programme.	1	2	3	4	5
Your brother or sister borrows something without asking.	1	2	3	4	5
Someone has messed up a model that you own.	1	2	3	4	5
Someone has taken your snack out of your drawer.	1	2	3	4	5
Another child has bullied you.	1	2	3	4	5

What would you do?

Two of your friends are arguing.

You see a bigger child push a smaller child in the playground.

You put a new small toy safely in your drawer. When you come back to it, you see that it is broken and know someone must have touched it.

You see someone in your class taking another child's snack out of their bag.

You see some people in the playground drawing graffiti on the wall.

You see some people in the school grounds after the school is closed.

One of your friends asks you not to talk to another friend because they have fallen out with them.

Your friends are calling another child an unkind name.

You know that two children are planning to have a fight at playtime.

Left, right

I **left** my house **right** on the stroke of noon. I know I was **right** about this because I heard the church clock strike twelve times. The church is **right** next to my house on the **left**-hand side of the road. I was pleased because there was plenty of time **left** before my train was due to depart from the platform on the **left**. I got into my car to drive to the railway station. My car is unusual as the steering wheel is on the **left**. Usually in this country, the steering wheel is on the **right** because we drive on the **left**-hand side of the road. I bought my car in France, and they drive on the **right**-hand side of the road there. I was halfway to the station when I realised that I had **left** my train ticket at home. I turned the car round **right** away and drove back to get it. Before I **left** the house again, my mother called from the garden, 'It's a good job your head is attached or you'd be finding that in the **left** luggage'.

'All **right**, very funny,' I said. I had just two minutes **left** when I reached the platform at the station. 'Phew, **right** on time,' I thought as the train **left** the station.

The mouse, the tree and the wind

There was once a tall **tree** in a grassy meadow. A small **mouse** lived in a hole at the bottom of the **tree**. When the **wind** blew, the **tree** swayed backwards and forwards and the **mouse** was worried that the **tree** might be blown down. A sudden movement by the **tree** woke the **mouse** one day. Oh my, he thought, the **tree** is swaying badly today. I hope the **wind** won't blow it down. The **mouse** left his hole in the **tree** to see what was happening. The **wind** was howling and the **tree** was bending this way and that. My poor **tree**, thought the **mouse**, this **wind** will surely blow my lovely **tree** down. Whatever shall I do? The **wind** howled and the **tree** shuddered. The **wind** shrieked and the **tree** shook. The **mouse** put his paws over his eyes. He was too scared to see what the **wind** was doing to the **tree**. Suddenly, the **wind** died down and the **tree** became still. The **mouse** breathed a sigh of relief that his **tree** was still standing. I'm glad the **wind** has gone and my **tree** is still here, thought the **mouse**, and he went back to his hole at the bottom of the **tree** and hoped for a quieter sleep.

Training and Resources
Available from Jenny Mosley Consultancies

For more information about training, contact Jenny Mosley Consultancies:
Telephone: 01225 767157
E-mail: circletime@jennymosley.co.uk
Website: www.circle-time.co.uk
Write to: 8 Westbourne Road, Trowbridge, Wiltshire, BA14 0AJ

Jenny Mosley's Whole School Quality Circle Time Model is now well established and welcomed by thousands of schools throughout the UK.

'In my long-time experience working in this field, I have not found anything that gives schools a structure and systems to support a whole school culture for emotional wellbeing that is as good as Jenny's Golden Model'.
Ian Read, *Headteacher, Watercliffe Meadow Primary School, Sheffield, November 2024*

In light of our current digital times, there is a resurgence of interest from teachers in how to support young people to be in the moment with others in a way that is respectful and positive.

Research proves that Games, Laughter and Fun boost the mental health of young people.

Jenny's courses are for all educators – headteachers, teachers, learning mentors, behaviour support teams, teaching assistants, educational psychologists, administrative support teams and many others.

Books to promote better behaviour

Mosley, J. (1996) *Quality Circle Time in the Primary Classroom: Your Essential Guide to Enhancing Self-Esteem, Self-Discipline and Positive Relationships*

Mosley, J. (1998) *More Quality Circle Time: Evaluating your Practice and Developing Creativity Within the Whole School Quality Circle Time Model*

Mosley, J. and Sonnet, H. (2005) *Better Behaviour through Golden Time: Practical Ideas for a Calm School Ethos*

Mosley, J. and Sonnet, H. (2026) *101 Games for Self-Esteem: Building Confidence and Motivation*

Mosley, J. and Sonnet, H. (2026) *101 Games for Social Skills: Exploring Positive Relationships and Healthy Interactions*

Mosley, J. and Sonnet, H. (2026) *101 Activities to Help Children Get On Together: Building Co-operation and Belonging*

Training options to promote better behaviour

- **Book Jenny Mosley Directly to Work with your Classes and Teachers**

Jenny can work with your school and challenging classes to help develop ways of building class discussion, social competencies and a respectful learning community with as many staff as possible observing – followed by debrief and end of day staff meeting.

Benefits – no cover or staff travel expenses and direct face to face training.

- **Book Jenny Mosley Directly to Work with your Midday Supervisors and TAs**

Jenny can work with Midday Supervisors and Teaching Assistants. Jenny would first hold a morning workshop covering many aspects of lunchtimes and playtimes then at lunchtime, go into your playground and work with your children and staff to observe and assess how your current initiatives are working. In the afternoon she will feed back a raft of ways forward to the staff and a senior manager.

Benefits – no Midday Supervisor cover needed as staff work over lunchtime and the day includes a workshop, consultancy and feedback.

- **Book Jenny Mosley for a Closure INSET Day for All Your Staff and Other Local Schools if you Choose**

If you are looking for Closure INSET day to build a whole staff vision and to work with the whole team on wellbeing and building resilience and respectful relationships with staff and children, then this is the right training day for you.

Benefits – the whole staff can reflect, engage and work together as a Team. The day includes games and fun activities that all the adults can use with children as well.

- **Limited Budget? Book Jenny's Training Webinar to Support Your Midday Supervisors**

If your budget is too stretched, then a Training Webinar is available on our website. It has downloadable booklets and a certificate that you can use for yourselves in staff meetings or can give out individually to Midday Supervisors.

For Product Safety Concerns and Information please contact our EU representative GPSR@taylorandfrancis.com
Taylor & Francis Verlag GmbH, Kaufingerstraße 24, 80331 München, Germany

www.ingramcontent.com/pod-product-compliance
Lightning Source LLC
Chambersburg PA
CBHW081229170426
43191CB00036B/2325